PRAISE FOR
STUMBLING INTO GRACE

"Lisa Harper is a mess. And I mean that in the best possible way, because, really—aren't we all? It's just that she isn't afraid to admit it, make you laugh about it, and give a good dose of hope along the way. And she has obviously been reading our (spiritual) mail. *Stumbling Into Grace* is a love letter to everyone who has ever felt like their personal brand of Christianity wasn't quite tidy enough, wasn't quite 'Christian' enough. We all long to come before the Lover of Our Souls like a spiritual ballerina, but more of us relate to a clumsy Dick Van Dyke style entrance (I know, I know . . . if you're under the age of 40, Google it). Lisa totally 'gets' the spiritual klutz inside all of us and reminds us how God's amazing grace not only covers our clumsy overtures but transforms us into grace-givers ourselves."

Anita Renfroe, comedian and author

"An author that can teach and explain solid Biblical foundations, provide life application of those statutes, and literally make you laugh out loud while doing so is a rare treasure. Well, give me a pirate hat and say 'Arrrr matie,' because I've hit the mother lode of all treasures! Lisa Harper's *Stumbling Into Grace* opened my eyes to truths in an entirely new way. I laughed, I cried, and I was challenged and refreshed. In the end, I was changed. You will be too."

Mandisa Hundley, gospel singer and *American Idol* alum

"This book brings together everything I love about Lisa. She is profound and hilarious, wise and wonderfully authentic. Every time I read Lisa's words or listen to her speak I am reminded of the simple truth that Christ invites us to lay down the burdens that are crushing us and take up the life he has promised to everyone who loves him. You will find yourself in these pages, but you might also find a depth of grace that will surprise you."

Sheila Walsh, author of *The Shelter of God's Promises*

"I love the way Lisa Harper tells stories, on the platform and on the page. Her style is engaging, her details ring true, and her message is clear. Lisa's fine grasp of Scripture and love for the Lord make her a trustworthy teacher, yet we learn from her own hard-earned lessons as well. She speaks and writes from a place of understanding, as she clings to God's hand, giving us the privilege of stumbling into grace with her. A wonderful book."

Liz Curtis Higgs, best-selling author of *Bad Girls of the Bible*

"In this book Lisa Harper shows us a reflection of who we all are, in one way or another. With her fabulous humor, she makes us laugh, and with her incredible insight she helps us learn more about the peace and love that Jesus offers. Lisa speaks grace, teaches grace and lives grace. She's my kind of woman! So if you want a little encouragement during what sometimes feels like just another long, difficult day, read this book. It'll lift your spirit."

Luci Swindoll, author and Women Of Faith speaker

"Wanna make my day? Give me Lisa Harper in any form. She's a dip in a pool, a tall glass of sweet tea, a pocketful of fun, and a sky-rocketing lift to my faith. Her gift of storytelling is mesmerizing. And her teacher's heart is evident and clear. Her wild antics only pale next to her sincere love for all things Jesus. From snakes to kittens, from dancing to death, you will find yourself repeatedly stumbling into grace. I did."

Patsy Clairmont, author of *Kaleidoscope* and
Women of Faith speaker

"I have been a fan of Lisa Harper for years and now so honored to call her friend. She has also been a mentor to me, although she would probably say 'not.' I have loved learning from her how she sees and then applies the truths found in God's Word. Lisa's newest book is all that and more. She not only stumbled her way into some grace, but she stumbled upon some powerful principles that help me be a better woman of God today."

Sandi Patty, most awarded female vocalist in
gospel music and author of *The Edge of the Divine*

"Okay, yes, *Stumbling Into Grace* is rich in significant content. It is real. It is theologically scholarly. It is engaging and enjoyable. It is sneakily profound. But, I have to admit, the reason I loved it so much is because it is so stinking funny! Lisa Harper is a delightful and hysterical writer. You will love her . . . and this book."

Lisa Whelchel, best-selling author of *Creative Correction*, *Friendship for Grownups*, and *The Facts of Life and Other Lessons My Father Taught Me*

"Lisa has a unique way of conversationally delivering divine truths. One minute you'll find yourself laughing so hard your sides are hurting and the tears are falling. In the next, you'll find that the tears have sprung from a deeper place; one that's leaking with the intent of healing and purifying you. All the while, Lisa makes us feel as if we are taking a stumble or even at times a graceful, grace-filled walk, with a good friend by our side."

Nicole C. Mullen, award-winning singer-songwriter

"It's such an honor to call Lisa Harper friend. She is honest and funny, wise and witty. And this book is just like Lisa—full of golden nuggets of Truth to tuck away in your heart and mind. I'm grateful that on these pages she has reminded me of the unconditional love of my Redeemer, and that the safest and greatest embrace is found in the arms of my Savior."

Natalie Grant, award-winning singer-songwriter

"Because I have the honor of knowing Lisa in person, I can imagine her eyes smiling as she shares life within these pages. As she shared about everything from pantyhose to deeply personal struggles, I found myself learning more and more about the God who blessed her with a tremendous gift and an extraordinary story. Her authentic and disarming candor fills the space between girlfriend and Bible teacher so effortlessly that you will see Scripture in a fresh, tangible way as you read. Lisa is able to articulate her love for Jesus in a way that will bless you not only as a reader, but as a fellow woman who might feel like she is stumbling into grace. We all want to live our faith lives well, and our shortcomings can seem overwhelming in a world where so many people try to make it look like they've got it together. Kudos and enormous gratitude to Lisa, who spoke for all of us 'sometimes spiritually clumsy' women. You are a rare treasure and I thank God we get to share a little corner of life."

Angie Smith, author of *I Will Carry You*

"Lisa is truly one of the most energetic and encouraging individuals I've ever met. Her passionate belief in God's specific love for each one of us helps me believe just a little more. Whether you're stumbling or all-out falling, Lisa reminds us through Scripture and story that grace is always waiting."

Kelly Minter, speaker, author, and worship leader

"After reading the intro, I realized that this book was an absolute and immediate must-read. So I decided to forgo my extended nap on my coast to coast flight and indulge. It was so worth it! Lisa has the ability to present such a profound gospel and magnificent, sovereign God in such an accessible way. She just makes it so clear. I enjoyed every section of every chapter. When I wasn't laughing, almost to the point of tears, I was being reminded of and inspired by our savior's amazing love and grace that he so freely gives us. I love this book!"

Tina Campbell, singer and songwriter of the #1 hit "Shackles" with Mary Mary

"If you've ever heard Lisa Harper teach in person, you've been endeared to her in your heart forever. Her storytelling is authentic, relatable, and humorous which makes her Bible teaching simple enough for a non-theological major (like me!) to understand. Lisa conveys the principles of each life lesson with such heart and insight that everyone can relate to them, no matter what our background or length of time walking in faith. *Stumbling Into Grace* captures honesty in the mishaps of life and brings us to a better understanding of our Father, our Creator, our Savior, our God and Friend."

Candace Cameron Bure, actress, speaker,

author of *New York Times* bestseller *Reshaping It All*

OTHER BOOKS
BY LISA HARPER

stumbling
INTO
grace

Confessions of a Sometimes
Spiritually Clumsy Woman

LISA
HARPER

THOMAS NELSON
Since 1798

NASHVILLE   DALLAS   MEXICO CITY   RIO DE JANEIRO

Published in Nashville, Tennessee, by Thomas Nelson. Thomas Nelson is a registered trademark of Thomas Nelson, Inc.

Author is represented by Anvil II Management, 12175 Network Blvd., Suite 150, San Antonio, TX 78249.

Thomas Nelson, Inc. titles may be purchased in bulk for educational, business, fund-raising, or sales promotional use. For information, please e-mail SpecialMarkets@ ThomasNelson.com.

Unless otherwise noted, Scripture quotations are taken from the Holy Bible, New International Version®, NIV®. © 1973, 1978, 1984, 2011 by Biblica, Inc.™ Used by permission of Zondervan. All rights reserved worldwide. www.zondervan.com

Scripture quotations marked ESV are from THE ENGLISH STANDARD VERSION. © 2001 by Crossway Bibles, a division of Good News Publishers.

Scripture quotations marked KJV are from the King James Version. Public domain.

Scripture quotations marked MSG are from *The Message* by Eugene H. Peterson. © 1993, 1994, 1995, 1996, 2000. Used by permission of NavPress Publishing Group. All rights reserved.

Scripture quotations marked NCV are from New Century Version®. © 2005 by Thomas Nelson, Inc. Used by permission. All rights reserved.

Scripture quotations marked NLT are from *Holy Bible*, New Living Translation. © 1996. Used by permission of Tyndale House Publishers, Inc., Wheaton, Illinois 60189. All rights reserved.

Page design by Mark L. Mabry

Library of Congress Cataloging-in-Publication Data

Harper, Lisa, 1963-
  Stumbling into grace : confessions of a sometimes spiritually clumsy woman / Lisa Harper.
    p. cm.
  Includes bibliographical references.
  ISBN 978-0-8499-4648-6 (trade paper)
  1. Harper, Lisa, 1963- 2. Christian biography. 3. Christian women--Religious life.
I. Title.
  BR1725.H23915 A3 2011
  277.3'082092--dc23
  [B]

                                                        2011017948

Printed in the United States of America

11 12 13 14 15 16 RRD 6 5 4 3 2 1

To Paige, Kelly, April, and Mary Katharine,
four dear friends who essentially lugged me to the
roof and lowered me to Jesus.

But God chose the foolish things of the world to shame the wise, and he chose the weak things of the world to shame the strong. He chose what the world thinks is unimportant and what the world looks down on and thinks is nothing in order to destroy what the world thinks is important. God did this so that no one can brag in his presence. Because of God you are in Christ Jesus, who has become for us wisdom from God. In Christ we are put right with God, and have been made holy, and have been set free from sin. So, as the Scripture says, "If people want to brag, they should brag only about the Lord."

—1 Corinthians 1:27–31 NCV

CONTENTS

Part 2: Real Gifts

Part 3: Real Growth

CONTENTS

ACKNOWLEDGMENTS

Special thanks to the Women of Faith and Thomas Nelson teams—especially my publisher, Matt Baugher—and the "Porch Pals" who've become one of my all-time favorite tribes! Also to my friends Peter and Pepper Magargee, who allowed their darling oldest daughter, Mary Holland, to grace the cover of this book.

introduction
WE HAD HIM AT "HELLO"

I passed a friend driving in the opposite direction on the road today. The moment I recognized her car, I began honking and waving (it was a slow speed zone); however, she drove on by completely oblivious to my friendly gyrations. Of course, she wasn't being intentionally aloof, but I still felt a tiny twinge of disappointment that she didn't notice me and that I didn't register as the smallest of blip on her radar.

Unfortunately, many people feel the same way about God. All too often humans assume they're invisible—or at least insignificant—when it comes to our Creator Redeemer. Not that they necessarily imagine God to be callous or cruel; they just figure He's so preoccupied with wars, famine, disease, natural disasters, slave trafficking, and Las Vegas that He doesn't have the time or emotional energy to notice what's going on in their wee corners of the world, much less care about it.

I beg to differ. I'm more convinced now than ever before

that we *matter* to God. He is intimately involved and infinitely interested in even the minutia of our lives. I believe it because I keep experiencing His tangible presence in the big and small spaces of my own life. And because of my vocation as a traveling Bible teacher, I've had the privilege of a proverbial box seat when it comes to watching our heavenly Father lovingly insert Himself into the lives of His unsuspecting children.

A recent observation took place at a retreat out West. I got to spend a three-day weekend with a small group of women, and we grew especially close after spending lots of time together praying, giggling, and groaning en masse while hiking up trails that would have made a mountain goat grouchy. In light of the bond we'd forged, I felt free to do something during our last session that I've never done before. I described some of the most painful chapters of my story, as well as how God had finally healed me from the shame that had plagued my heart and mind for most of my life. Then, after talking about how important it is for us to have figurative *Ebenezers* (literally translated "stone of help" in I Samuel 7:12 because it was a rock symbolizing the divine assistance Jehovah gave the Israelites during battles with their enemies) to help us remember the worth we have in Christ and break the bondage of degrading lies we've believed about ourselves, I asked anyone who had experienced physical or sexual abuse to stand up.

I wish I could tell you I was surprised when about half of the room stood. I can tell you for a split second I felt pulled by a riptide of panic and thought, *Oh, good night, what should I do now?* (There have been situations in the past when I thought God was impressing me to do something in a group setting only to realize later it was more likely a reaction to drinking too much caffeine or eating too much sugar; therefore, I'm wary of responding hastily when the Holy Spirit pokes me!) But in the very next instant, I calmly sensed God's Spirit prompting me to speak His truth directly to each woman standing. So I turned to the first girl to my left and said, "You are *not* stupid." Then I turned to the next and said, "You are *not* ugly." Then I turned to the third woman and paused, because she was the person I'd connected with the most that weekend. In a mere three days, she'd become a true friend. Plus, she was the group leader and a Bible teacher deeply respected in their community.

Our eyes held for a few seconds before I declared slowly and decisively, "Laura. You. Are. *Not*. Dirty." At which, she gasped and covered her mouth with her hand. For the next several minutes, I continued speaking words of affirmation and promises from Scripture over those brave, internally bruised warriors, such as, "There is therefore now no condemnation for those who are in Christ Jesus" (Romans 8:1 ESV). And, "No longer will they call you Deserted, / or name your land Desolate. / But you will be called Hephzibah, [which means "God's delight is in her"] / and your land Beulah [which means "married"]; / . . . as a bridegroom rejoices over his bride, / so will your God rejoice over you" (Isaiah 62:4–5). After I'd spoken directly to all the women standing, and we shared a sweet time of worship and Communion, there was a closing prayer, and everyone began dispersing in small chattering clumps.

Except for Laura, who edged her way over to me. After the chattering quieted down, she explained that she had been sexually molested by her uncle from the age of eight to the age of fifteen and that she'd graduated from high school early and gone out of state to college to escape his abuse. Most of the sadness left her eyes when she talked about meeting her husband, Paul, and how they had become Christians early in their marriage. She described how God had used both Paul's patience and Christian counseling to help her work through the painful memories of her childhood and adolescence. She went on to describe how grateful she was to have a good marriage and three precious little boys now.

Then she said softly, "You know, I almost didn't stand up tonight, because I was afraid someone might wonder if Paul had been abusive to me. Plus, I really thought I was over all that. But I couldn't stop thinking about that place deep inside my soul that still feels dirty every time Paul and I are physically intimate. So I stood up."

She said she was surprised when I began speaking directly to each woman standing. I told her I was a little surprised myself, because I'd never done so before and certainly hadn't planned the exercise. We both smiled; then Laura continued, "After you told the girl she wasn't ugly, I started praying, 'Oh God, please, *please* have Lisa tell me I'm not dirty, because then I'll know it's really coming from

You.' Right then you turned to me and said my name—you know, I'm the only one you called by name—and said those *exact* words. For the first time I can remember, I feel completely clean!" Of course, by then we both had tears streaming down our faces. Projectile crying is probably more accurate.

Laura's divine bath reminded me that God doesn't just *see* us; He *gazes adoringly* at us. He doesn't simply *notice* us; He *moves heaven and earth* on our behalf. That's the thesis of *Stumbling Into Grace*. The following pages describe God's unconditional and miraculously accessible love for us through the life and ministry of Jesus Christ. This is a collection of real-life stories (many from my "most embarrassing" list) and gospel stories—sort of a diary/devotional—proving that even on our worst days, we had Him at hello. I hope you find yourself laughing out loud a few times while reading this book—that turning the pages will feel more like a vacation than a chore—but I also hope you'll ponder the questions at the end of each chapter, maybe even with a friend or small group, because I think they can help Christ's affection become more of a personal reality than an ephemeral, ethereal concept.

My goal—which is for this lisping prose to compel readers to lean further into the strong, safe embrace of our Redeemer—is an incredibly lofty one. I know only by the empowerment of God's Spirit will it accomplish anything close to that. But one can hope and pray!

Warmest regards,
Lisa Harper

part 1
REAL LIFE

chapter 1
EWE SCARED?

Why is God doing this? Though it is blasphemous to think it,
our whole being cries out that this is unfair of him, that our grief
and pain are disproportionate to our sin, that we have been
abandoned.[1]

—D. A. Carson

So, today I've been thinking about scary things.

It all started with a phone call from my doctor. Actually, I should probably back up a bit further in my story and explain that I was raised in a family where you pretty much had to slice an artery before going to the doctor. No missing school because of the sniffles for us, though coughing up blood might qualify for skipping homeroom. Much as parents lecture their unappreciative offspring with tales of hiking through snowdrifts and milking seventeen cows before eating breakfasts of gruel, I'm tempted to lecture some of my seemingly wimpy friends about the dangers of hypochondria, which is why I was really flustered by my response to this recent phone call from my dermatologist.

I wasn't initially alarmed when her number appeared on my cell phone screen, not that she'd ever called before. I mean, we don't play tennis or belong to the same book club or anything. Our interaction has been limited to her peering at suspicious moles and making soothing small talk while I perch awkwardly on a narrow steel table and try to keep a Kleenex-sized paper gown from exposing my other parts. But I was expecting a call from her *office*, because her nurse had informed me the previous week that they would call when they got the results of a biopsy she'd had done on a weird, bumpy "rash" that had been coming and going above my right ear for several years. I wasn't expecting *Dr. Vincent's voice* when I picked up. I assumed it was the receptionist or maybe some nurse who drew the short stick that day and had to make phone calls instead of doing cool stuff like stabbing people with syringes or freezing warts.

The moment I recognized the doctor's voice, I knew the "rash" wasn't the psoriasis my former dermatologist had diagnosed. (Frankly, that threw me off my game for a while, because he made me use prescription shampoo that caused me to smell like a mechanic. Plus, he performed a lot of liposuction in addition to mole gazing, and I was afraid every time he examined me he was going to suggest I get my cellulite sucked out.) And while Dr. Vincent spoke several reassuring sentences before saying the "C" word, all I heard was, "Waah, waah, waah, waah, waah, *you have cancer!*"

Then Dr. Vincent explained that, although they couldn't know the extent of the growth until it was surgically removed, it was the *best* kind of skin cancer to have and was more than likely contained. What I heard was, "There is a disgusting mass upside your head that's probably leaking poison into your brain right now!"

The doctor finally assured me that the surgical scar would be hidden underneath my hair. I heard, "You're going to look like the bride of Frankenstein and a mob of angry citizens carrying pitchforks and lanterns is going to chase you out of your village in the middle of the night."

Of course, I didn't utter any of those crazy concerns out loud to Dr. Vincent. I was completely rational and very polite throughout the phone call. But after we said good-bye, I pulled over into a Walgreens parking lot and began to cry. A few minutes later, I called one of my closest friends and broke the news. She told me not to worry and reminded me that she'd had two carcinomas removed from her chest and was doing fine now. Then she said she loved me but had to go because she was in the middle of fixing dinner. Since I've been such a stoic patient in the past and preferred to hole up alone with Sprite and saltines during flu bouts, I was surprised by my sudden need for compassion. I realized, with an embarrassed start, that I had wanted Kim to gasp and dissolve into empathetic sobs. I became acutely aware that I was *scared*.

The truth is, I've struggled with fear my whole life. I've

only recently begun to pull it out from under the rug of denial. As a child, I was afraid my parents' divorce was at least partly my fault. Not too long after they split up, I became afraid of being permanently stained and unworthy after being sexually molested. I've been afraid of being abandoned by people who love me for as long as I can remember. I was afraid of disappointing my teachers in school, my professors in college, and my bosses at work. In my thirties, I began to be afraid of being single for the rest of my life. I really didn't want to end up as the weird lady in the neighborhood who lived in squalor with only cats for company.

I've also burned up way too much emotional energy being afraid of not being good enough, sweet enough, thin enough, or spiritual enough. And I've been especially anxious about being perceived as afraid, because I always assumed being afraid was a *bad thing*. However, I'm discovering that being afraid is simply a *people thing*. Middle age and an increased awareness of my own frailty have teamed up to convince me that fear is an inexorable part of the human condition.

For example, I was in group therapy with a guy last year who is an officer in the military. He's been part of an elite Special Forces unit for more than twenty years and has participated in combat in two wars on two different continents. He has numerous medals and commendations for bravery. And he looks the part of an American hero too. He has a square jaw, broad shoulders, and biceps that strain the seams of his shirts. Yet after a week of intense counseling, his steely veneer shattered and tears rolled down his cheeks as he confessed how scared he was of never measuring up to his dad's expectations.

Besides soldiers with father issues, I've met performers who get shaky knees and dry mouths just prior to going onstage, young moms who worry about whether or not they can truly bond with their babies, brilliant CEOs who battle swarms of internal butterflies at the thought of being downsized, and more than a few preachers terrified to admit their own sins. I don't think anyone is exempt from being at least momentarily frightened of something or someone. Whether based on an actual threat, such as a cancer diagnosis, or on some imaginary boogieman hiding in the basement, we all have fears. The good news is that we also have a Shepherd who is particularly tender with trembling sheep.

Jesus provides security during the scariest chapters of our stories.

JESUS AND SCARY THINGS

Then Jesus said to his disciples: "Therefore I tell you, do not worry about your life, what you will eat; or about your body, what you will wear. Life is more than food, and the body more than clothes. Consider the ravens: They do not sow or reap, they have no storeroom or barn; yet God feeds them. And how much more valuable you are than birds! Who of you by worrying can add a single hour to your life? Since you cannot do this very little thing, why do you worry about the rest?

"Consider how the lilies grow. They do not labor or spin. Yet I tell you, not even Solomon in all his splendor was dressed like one of these. If that is how God clothes the grass of the field, which is here today, and tomorrow is thrown into the fire, how much more will he clothe you, O you of little faith! And do not set your heart on what you will eat or drink; do not worry about it. For the pagan world runs after all such things, and your Father knows that you need them. But seek his kingdom, and these things will be given to you as well.

"Do not be afraid, little flock, for your Father has been pleased to give you the kingdom." (Luke 12:22–32 UPDATED NIV)

The Heart of His Story

I used to wonder why we had four different Gospel accounts in the Bible—Matthew, Mark, Luke, and John. They all narrate the same basic timeline of Jesus' life and earthly ministry. So why didn't Matt, Marco, Johnny, and the Doc just meet at a local coffee shop with their laptops, brainstorm about what they had observed, and create a single literary masterpiece? Why four different versions of the same story?

Professors in seminary gave me multisyllabic academic answers to that question, but my all-time-favorite explanation came from an enthusiastic Vacation Bible School teacher we had when I was about ten or eleven years old. She told us to imagine four different people, standing on four different street corners, watching the same parade.

Then she said, "What do you think would happen if you got those four people together after the parade and asked them to describe what they saw?"

If memory serves me correctly, several hands shot up along with exclamations of, "Oooooh, oooooh, oooooh, I know!"

Then one of us blurted out that they would have described the parade differently because they had observed it from individual viewpoints. Our teacher nodded and explained that's what the first four books of the New Testament were like. Four different guys, observing the "parade" of Christ's life and ministry from four different vantage points, and then describing what they saw. Consequently, we have four wonderfully nuanced gospels, each having a distinctive purpose and flavor:

Matthew's purpose was to give his readers treasures, and his flavor is decidedly Jewish since he preached to a mostly Jewish audience.

Mark's purpose was to declare the *good news* of Jesus to the whole world (the word *gospel* comes from the Greek word *euangelion*, which means "a decree of good news." Mark was also the first writer to associate *gospel* with the Messiah), and his flavor is energetic.

John's purpose was passionately evangelistic (John 20:31), and his flavor is bold.

Luke's purpose was to help believers grow in their faith, and his flavor—probably like his bedside manner as a physician—is compassionate.[2] And since I'm a sucker for anything soft, Luke tends to be my go-to guy. That's why I love Luke's repetition of the Sermon on the Mount (recorded in Matthew 5–7; Luke 6) here in chapter 12. If you're familiar with Christ's homily on a hill, you probably noticed that Dr. Luke edited the original sermon with a few unique additions and deletions of his own, a habit most good storytellers have. In fact, his use of the term *little flock* in verse 32 is so unique that this is the only place it can be found in the entire Bible. The phrase Luke coined comes from a double diminutive word coupling in Greek and can literally be translated "little, little flock."

Most commentaries skip right over that tender title and focus on the meat of Christ's message here, which was an admonition about being fearful, a how-to manual on trusting God with our financial portfolios and our physical health, and a warning against worrying. It's a practical sermon filled with great truisms we need to be tutored in over and over again: God will provide our needs. God will protect us. He has control over our bodies and our bank accounts. However, from where I'm standing, the affectionate pet name at the end of this passage is what really drives the Messiah's point home: "little, little flock." Only a Shepherd, who absolutely adores His sheep, would use that phrase. And that's the Shepherd I'll run to when I'm scared.

Hope for Our Ongoing Stories

I was back at the hospital today, but not for the basal cell carcinoma Dr. Vincent discovered lurking above my right ear. Thankfully, a surgeon was able to remove that whole "rash," and the resulting Frankenstein scar is only visible if I wear a hair fountain, which doesn't look that good on adults anyway. This morning's appointment was much more routine in nature. I went to the Centennial Women's Health Center in downtown Nashville to have my tah-tahs squashed (usually referred to as a mammogram by people with a sense of propriety).

After I signed in, a big nurse came out to greet me. She called me "honey" throughout the registration process and the walk back to the flattening area. The tiny droplets of fear that had rolled into my mind in the waiting room evaporated at the tenderness of her tone. And every time she said "honey," my heart turned up at the corners. It reminded me of the nickname Jesus gave us two thousand years ago: *Don't be afraid, little, little ewes.* It reminded me that we have a gentle, protective, and ever-present Shepherd.

Living in Light of His Story

Dear Jesus, help me cling to You when I'm afraid, instead of hiding in the dark by myself. Teach me to trust You no matter how scary my journey gets. I want to find my greatest treasure in Your constant presence. Amen.

Personal Reflection and/or Group Discussion Questions

1. What are three physical, tangible things you're afraid of (e.g., spiders, snakes, clowns)?

2. What are three emotional, less tangible things you're afraid of (e.g., abandonment, conflict, being misunderstood)?

3. When it comes to admitting fear, on the scale of one to ten below—with one being "stoic" and ten being "scaredy-cat"—circle the number that represents where you would place yourself:

   1   2   3   4   5   6   7   8   9   10

4. What do you think your closest friends and family would say are your greatest fears?

5. Describe a recent experience that really scared you.

6. Reread Luke 12:32. What does Jesus' term of endearment "little flock" mean to you in this season of your life?

7. Read Isaiah 43:1–3. How would you condense the theme of these verses into a song or movie title?

8. What's one practical thing you can begin doing today to apply that theme to your own life?

Journal Entry

Please consider completing this sentence in your personal journal:

So, today I've been thinking about what I'm really afraid of, Jesus, and . . .

chapter 2
THE VERY REAL PROBLEM
WITH PANTYHOSE

For a compassionate man nothing human is alien: no joy and no
sorrow, no way of living and no way of dying . . . This compassion
pulls people away from the fearful clique into the large world where
they can see that every human face is the face of a neighbor.[1]

—Henri Nouwen

So, today I've been thinking about binding things.

The thought flitted around my mind and then landed for a while, likely because I was wearing a pair of too-tight jeans. But as I shifted uncomfortably on the couch and pondered whether I really needed to go to the restroom or whether these pants were simply squeezing my bladder, I realized my aversion to confinement can be traced back to a pair of pantyhose.

They weren't even *my* hose; they were part of the ensemble my second cousin Brenda was wearing one Sunday night when we were thirteen years old. She had dressed up especially nice that evening, because she was to be the first of several of us who were going to speak about our experience at church camp. A few minutes before the worship service began, a serious deacon ushered us to the very front pew where a lone microphone loomed menacingly. Then, after an organ prelude and a few hymns, the pastor introduced us, and Brenda stood bravely, turned to face the congregation, and began.

She barely glanced at the notes she'd written neatly. Her voice rang out strong and true in the Missionary Alliance Church sanctuary. Some of her poise was due to the fact that it was the church she'd grown up in. These were her people. Plus, she was the star of the youth group. She volunteered at Vacation Bible School, she memorized lots of Scripture verses, and she sincerely liked the scary rapture movies the youth pastor forced us to watch. The rest of us plopped on that pew were jittery ruffians by comparison. Worse still, I was a known interloper, who went to their CMA summer camp and some of their youth group activities, but was actually a member of the big, pink Baptist church across the street.

Thirtysomething years later, I still don't know what came over me. One minute I was sitting in front of Brenda, listening intently to her explain how God had impacted her at Lake Swan Camp, and the next minute I had freed my right foot from a shiny dress shoe and was pulling on her pantyhose with my "pincher toes." (I was born with the enviable gift of grasping things between my big toe and the one next to it, much like a monkey.)

I can still remember Brenda's look of horror and confusion: *why in the world is Lisa sabotaging my testimony by dragging my hose down with her nasty foot?* And I still feel terrible about it. Brenda's mom—my great aunt Paulene—was sitting just a few pews away from the action and although she couldn't actually see what I was doing, she assumed by my placement and personality that I was the cause of her daughter's decomposition.

She was fit to be tied when Brenda confirmed my naughtiness after the fact and called my mom (who'd been her favorite niece prior to this partial disrobing incident) when they got home. Of course, Mom was absolutely horrified to hear about my unprecedented behavior. I can't remember the exact consequences but I was punished sufficiently enough that I've never been tempted to pinch anyone in church with my toes since. And while I dutifully performed the additional penance Mom meted out and apologized profusely to everyone involved, it's still an embarrassing blip in both my personal and family history.

There was just something about those hose that made me snap. All these years later, I still hate pantyhose. I actually don't like *anything* that confines. Well, except for Spanx when I'm in a chubby season, and this killer pair of thigh-high boots I bought last year. Perhaps I should rephrase. I don't like constraints that limit the ability to have authentic relationships with God and each other.

But I wasn't always such a free spirit. I've spent the better part of my life dutifully trying to draw inside the "good Christian" lines superimposed by popular American conservative evangelical culture. Among other things, that meant I tried to go to church every Sunday and most Wednesday nights (and was riddled with guilt if I didn't); tried to avoid R-rated movies and rock music (and was riddled with guilt if I didn't); tried to read the Bible through in a year, every year (and was riddled with guilt if I didn't); tried to have at least a twenty-minute "quiet time" alone with God every single morning (and was riddled with guilt if I didn't); and tried to act positive and normal about accosting strangers on the beach, in the park, and on planes with the terribly intrusive question: "Do you know, if you died tonight, that you'd go to heaven?" so as to please my evangelism training leader (and was riddled with both guilt and class condemnation if I didn't).

In my experience, liberty and authenticity can be problematic if you're a Christ-follower who doesn't live alone in a cabin in the woods stocked with good coffee, dark chocolate, and cable television. That's because, since the beginning of biblical history, people of faith have attached rules and conditions—far beyond the directives God gives us in Scripture—to our belief systems. The heavenly Father's precious children—filthy scoundrels all of us, apart from His mercy—seem intent on making each other miserable. Nylon leg coverings are just the tip of the legalistic iceberg.

Don't even get me started about hair buns, embroidered Bible covers, and high-necked shirts.

In light of the juxtaposition between Jesus' words in the gospel of John, which says, "So if the Son sets you free, you will be free indeed" (John 8:36), and the humorless rigidity so often demonstrated by believers, I sometimes wonder why He doesn't zap a wormhole from glory to here and bellow, "*If you don't stop that right now, I'm gonna be on you like white on rice!*" Of course, Jesus would probably use a more majestic, less folksy warning than my dad. But still, don't you wonder what He would say about all the confining junk we lug around and label "spiritual"?

Jesus provides freedom, regardless of what's been cramping our stories.

Jesus and Binding Things

At that time Jesus was walking through some fields of grain on a Sabbath day. His followers were hungry, so they began to pick the grain and eat it. When the Pharisees saw this, they said to Jesus, "Look! Your followers are doing what is unlawful to do on the Sabbath day."

Jesus answered, "Have you not read what David did when he and the people with him were hungry? He went into God's house, and he and those with him ate the holy bread, which was lawful only for priests to eat. And have you not read in the law of Moses that on every Sabbath day the priests in the Temple break this law about the Sabbath day? But the priests are not wrong for doing that. I tell you that there is something here that is greater than the Temple. The Scripture says, 'I want kindness more than I want animal sacrifices.' You don't really know what those words mean. If you understood them, you would not judge those who have done nothing wrong.

"So the Son of Man is Lord of the Sabbath day."

Jesus left there and went into their synagogue, where there was a man with a crippled hand. They were looking for a reason to accuse Jesus, so they asked him, "Is it right to heal on the Sabbath day?"

Jesus answered, "If any of you has a sheep, and it falls into a ditch on the Sabbath day, you will help it out of the ditch. Surely a human being is more important than a sheep. So it is lawful to do good things on the Sabbath day."

Then Jesus said to the man with the crippled hand, "Hold out your hand." The man held out his hand, and it became well again, like the other hand. But the Pharisees left and made plans to kill Jesus. (Matthew 12:1–14 NCV)

The Heart of His Story

While I'm tempted to insist that Jesus doesn't like pantyhose either, I will concede that's a bit of a stretch (no pun intended). But it's not overreaching to say Jesus didn't like the oppressive regulations that often accompany religious devotion. And this incident in Matthew is a good example of His disregard for legalism, especially when it is valued more than people.

Christ's overall theme of grace and liberty is actually present in the seemingly insignificant first three words of this story. Because the short phrase *at that time* is like literary Velcro; it attaches what's happening in chapter 12 to what just took place in chapter 11 when our Savior tenderly promised to give rest to those who are tired and worn out from carrying heavy burdens (Matthew 11:28–30). That means Jesus and His disciples are hiking through this field of ripe grain within days, or maybe just hours, after His promise of relief for the weary. And that's when the Twelve began to snap off some wheat or barley and chew it to silence their growling stomachs.

It's understandable that the disciples would experience physical hunger, since they were itinerant evangelists without steady paychecks or mealtimes. What strikes me as unusual is the Pharisees' proximity; they were close enough to observe the disciples snacking. You probably remember that Pharisees were prominent leaders in orthodox Jewish society during Christ's earthly ministry. They were responsible for interpreting the Torah—the Hebrew Scriptures—into a comprehensive list of behavioral guidelines, so they spent most of their time in the temple or neighborhood synagogues. The image of them traipsing through a field, spying on a motley crew of Christ-followers, implies they were not only out of their element, but they were up to no good.

Now I'm sure some of the Pharisees were well intentioned, sincerely believing they could get closer to God through ritual purity. History reveals there were even a few truly good men among them; Nicodemus became a real worshipper after a life-changing nocturnal visit with Jesus, and Joseph of Arimathea petitioned Pilate for Christ's body after He died on the cross and then tithed his own tomb to ensure Jesus had a proper burial. But for the most part, their passion for religious minutia robbed them of compassion for and genuine relationship with "regular" folks who weren't as fastidious. In fact, the Greek word translated "Pharisee" in the New Testament is *Pharisaios*, which literally means "separate ones."[2] And in light of the way this particular group pounced on the first chance they had to condemn Christ and His followers, it's obvious their intentions came from crooked hearts.

However, the Messiah refuted their angry accusation with the actual interpretation of the scripture they were twisting to fit their own agenda. He reminded them about the divinely ordained provision of food in the case of David and in priestly ceremony, both of which illustrated God putting human needs above strict adherence to written law or rabbinical tradition. Then Jesus added that God wants kindness more than He wants animal sacrifices. In other words, God wants us to care about people more than we care about policies and appearance. He wants us to focus on *loving* more than we focus on *looking spiritual*. The Son of God concluded by proclaiming His authority over the Sabbath, the day of rest His Father established for us.

Almost as if to demonstrate His proclamation, Jesus then cut across the field and strode into a synagogue—the very place they practiced Sabbath. Once they caught up to

Him and elbowed their way to the front of the crowd that had gathered, the Pharisees singled out a man with a withered hand and asked, "What do You think about healing this guy right here, right now, Jesus?" Mind you, their sarcastic query wasn't a fluke. There was a well-established principle in Jewish tradition that physical healing, which was regarded as *work*, was forbidden on the Sabbath, except in life-threatening situations.[3] And since this man wasn't in danger of dying, the Pharisees callously picked him as bait to trap Jesus.

In my imagination, Jesus regarded those zealous legalists with a slow, sad smile. Then He patiently explained that, since there are exceptions for pulling a stranded animal out of a ditch on the Sabbath, surely it's all right with our Father in heaven when we extend kindness to a man, woman, or child. As those ancient deacons stood there grimacing, unsure of how to retort, Jesus healed the disfigured man. No doubt everyone in the synagogue was dumbfounded by the supernatural demonstration of Christ's deity. And I'll bet a select few were also red-faced, having had their misinterpretation of God's will so publicly exposed.

Hope for Our Ongoing Stories

Church, the setting in which most of us now practice Sabbath, is one of God's many gracious provisions for human frailty. He knows we are prone to wander and need to be reminded of His goodness and faithfulness. So our Creator provided a divine pit stop—whether we go to a theater with cup-holders presided over by a man in skinny jeans on Saturday night, or to an elegant room ringed with stained-glass windows that's presided over by a woman in a robe on Sunday morning—wherein we can have our souls refueled by worshiping Him and hanging out with other limping, like-minded disciples. It was never meant to be a prescribed time and place for us to obsess about doing the appropriate thing at the appropriate moment all while wearing an appropriate outfit.

Ultimately, I think when believers gather it would be more God-honoring if we functioned as a medical center instead of a country club. Wouldn't it be awesome if everybody wore hospital gowns, complete with the requisite gap in the back, and had to choose either a wheelchair or crutches as our mode of transportation before entering the sanctuary? It might just help us remember that we're all sick and in desperate need of the medicine only Jesus provides.

Living in Light of His Story

Dear Jesus, please forgive me for being a modern-day Pharisee and for often being more concerned about how spiritual I look instead of how to love other image-bearers well. I need Your Spirit to slay my attempts to justify myself and remind me that my only hope is in You. I also need Your Spirit to tutor me in the practice of Sabbath, of resting all my attention and affection on You. Thank You for fresh mercy this morning, and help me to live today in heightened awareness of Your words: "For I have come to call not those who think they are righteous, but those who know they are sinners" (Matthew 9:13 NLT). Amen.

Personal Reflection and/or Group Discussion Questions

1. Do you tend to be more of a rule-follower or a rule-breaker?

2. What are a few rules and conditions, beyond those you think God commands in Scripture, to which religious authority figures (perhaps well-intentioned) have attempted to get you to conform to in the past?

3. Have you ever rebelled against what you considered to be unbiblical regulations? If so, how did you "push back"?

4. Why do you think the Pharisees put more energy into legalistically adhering to religious guidelines than in loving the needy people all around them?

5. Describe some ways you've observed a healthy church (or individual Christians) giving people priority over policies.

6. Read 1 Corinthians 8:9–13 and 9:19–23. Describe a chapter in your story when you chose to follow rules you didn't really *have to* as a Christian, in order to better reflect God's love to someone who was more behaviorally conservative. How do you think "stumbling block" theology is most often distorted or manipulated?

7. Read John 8:36. What are three specific areas in your life where you would like to experience more freedom (e.g., being more demonstrative in worship, taking dancing lessons)?

Journal Entry

Please consider completing this sentence in your personal journal:

So, today I've been thinking about areas in my life where I need more liberty, Jesus, and . . .

chapter 3
TAKE A LOAD OFF

Addictions are ultimately a disorder of worship. Will we worship ourselves and our own desires, or will we worship the true God?[1]
—Edward T. Welch

So, today I've been thinking about fattening things.

I must confess, I derive a lot of pleasure from chewing and swallowing the kinds of foods that cause one to be fluffy. There aren't too many things I enjoy more than a hearty meal or a heavy snack. Unfortunately, *tasty* and *fattening* have been purged from my vocabulary lately, because I just finished a three-week, five-hundred-calorie-a-day fast in which I wasn't allowed to eat bread or dairy or processed sugar or fat of any kind.

I wasn't supposed to drink caffeine either. However, I

told the holistic nurse who supervised this "toxin cleanse" that, if she expected me to go twenty-one days without eating a piece of yummy whole-grain bread, or enjoying my beloved goat cheese with apple slices, or drizzling olive oil on steamed vegetables, or savoring one tiny dark-chocolate-covered almond, then she would simply have to allow me a few ounces of Diet Coke every afternoon. That is, unless she wanted me to be cleansed of sanity too!

I don't know if you've ever tried to subsist on one grape-fruit, five strawberries, six paper-thin slices of turkey, and twelve asparagus spears per day for almost a month, but I found it to be quite taxing. I became light-headed within the first twenty-four hours and within forty-eight hours I found myself wandering around the house aimlessly or slouching on the couch staring off into space, because evidently I wasn't eating enough to fuel basic brain activity.

By the third day, my stomach had hardened into a tiny, angry, acidic knot, and my legs trembled when I walked up or down stairs. Then I started seeing stars and brilliant bursts of white light when I ran. Of course, the nurse had advised against doing anything more strenuous than walking during the course of the diet because of the severe caloric restriction, but I thought maybe running would help me forget the fact that I was starving. Plus, I've read that physical exercise releases the same endorphins as having sex does, and being a single, celibate, middle-aged, desperately hungry woman, I figured I could use all the endorphins I could get.

At the end of the first week of this self-imposed fast, a

dear friend gently questioned my capacity to continue nibbling like a supermodel for two more weeks and said she
thought I should immediately head to Wendy's for a cheeseburger. I think she was alarmed that I was sitting across
from her in Starbucks weeping softly with a white-knuckled
grip on a cup of Splenda-sweetened green tea. With eyebrows knit together in concern, she then asked if I was sure
it was God who had convicted me to limit my food intake.

Interestingly enough, He hadn't. I didn't choose to cut
certain foods and drinks from my diet for spiritual reasons.
God didn't *tell me* to fast last month. Frankly, I've always
subscribed to my friend Lisa Whelchel's food philosophy,
because she insists that if Jesus hadn't wanted us to eat carbohydrates, He wouldn't have referred to Himself as the
"Bread of Life"! I just wanted to be a little more responsible
about what I was putting into my body. I reasoned that now
that I'm in my late forties, it'd probably be a good idea to
be more intentional about maintaining my health by eating
cleaner, less-processed, lower-fat foods. Plus, I had several
pairs of really cute jeans hanging in my closet that were too
tight, and I assumed that following a caloric-restrictive diet
for a while might help me lose a few pounds and squeeze
back into them.

Little did I know how very spiritual the fast would
become, because the light-headedness soon gave way to
an elevated sense of awareness. Having an empty stomach
actually led to a less-cluttered heart and mind. Without
the distraction of Frappucinos and french fries, I quickly
realized there were more toxins clogging my *soul* than there

were triglycerides clogging my arteries. The extra weight I was carrying in my spirit was much more dangerous than the fluff I was carrying around my hips and waist. And just as I numb my body's need for healthy nourishment when I gorge on junk food, I had also numbed my soul's need for confession—for *cleansing*—when I stuffed myself full of me-first rationalism.

When I stepped on the scales a few days ago, the arrow was pointing to a number twenty-three pounds less than it did a few months ago. It's the weight I used to lie about on my driver's license back when state governments imposed such indignities. I can now wear those darling boot-cut jeans that used to cut off my circulation. Mind you, they're not "skinny" jeans by fashion magazine standards, but I didn't buy them in the plus-size department either. And of course, I have more energy, more stamina, and stronger nails. (Actually, I'm not sure about the fingernail part, but that's what the brochure advertising this particular diet promised.)

More importantly, for the moment my heart feels significantly lighter. It's not weighed down by emotional fatty deposits like, *Why do I always have to be the one who says "I'm sorry" first?* Or *He should ask me out instead of her because, even though she has a better figure, I'm nicer and way more fun.* Or *If God isn't going to give me a husband and children, why doesn't He at least bless me with a best-selling book, a high metabolism, and small pores?* Today—well, at least this morning—those kinds of toxic thoughts that sometimes clog my soul are gone. I am fasting from whiny narcissism and a sense of entitlement. Right now

I'm content just being a sturdy, mistake-prone girl who is absolutely adored by a perfect Redeemer!

Jesus provides a heart-healthy cleanse that helps us jettison pounds of unattractive, jiggling pride.

JESUS AND FATTENING THINGS

> Now great crowds accompanied him, and he turned and said to them, "If anyone comes to me and does not hate his own father and mother and wife and children and brothers and sisters, yes, and even his own life, he cannot be my disciple." (Luke 14:25–26 ESV)

The Heart of His Story

This is one of the more concise yet ostensibly cruel declarations Jesus made to the throng of people who had begun following Him wherever He went. It's hard not to wonder if some bumbling admirer had stepped on His robe one too many times or a fan with ADD had exasperated Him with one too many words. The Son of God seems to have lost His cool, if not His compassion. He even seems to be contradicting the law His Father gave Moses: "You shall not hate your brother in your heart, but you shall reason frankly with your neighbor, lest you incur sin because of him" (Leviticus 19:17 ESV) with His semantic severity. But when we back up and look at the *analogy of Scripture* (using the entirety of God's Word to interpret individual passages), it becomes apparent that Jesus was referring to the cost of discipleship, not advocating fisticuffs with family members! And the proper context for His verbal bombshell in Luke 14 can be found in an Old Testament story about a couple of guys who desperately needed to drop a few pounds:

> Now Eli's sons were evil men; they did not care about the LORD. This is what the priests would normally do to the people: Every time someone brought a sacrifice, the meat would be cooked in a pot. The priest's servant would then come carrying a fork that had three prongs. He would plunge the fork into the pot or the kettle. Whatever the fork brought out of the pot belonged to the priest. But this is how they treated all the Israelites who came to Shiloh to offer sacrifices. Even before the fat was burned, the priest's servant would come to the person offering sacrifices and say, "Give the priest some meat to roast. He won't accept boiled meat from you, only raw meat."
>
> If the one who offered the sacrifice said, "Let the fat be burned up first as usual, and then take anything you want," the priest's servant would answer, "No, give me the meat now. If you don't, I'll take it by force."
>
> The LORD saw that the sin of the servants was very great because they did not show respect for the offerings made to the LORD. (1 Samuel 2:12–17 NCV)

Eli's sons, Hophni and Phinehas, made God their side dish instead of their entrée. As "junior priests" they were called and commissioned to treat the Israelite meat sacrifices with reverence and respect. And while as full-time temple employees they were allowed a portion of the ceremonial meat, they were supposed to receive it through a sort of holy "potluck" ritual, wherein they stabbed a big fork into a vat, and whatever it brought up was what they got to eat. However, these piggy priests decided to boycott the fondue system and began accosting worshippers before they entered the temple, demanding an animal protein entry fee. Instead of humbly bowing to God's specifications for how to handle sacrifices, they set up a barbecue pit in the churchyard and demanded prime cuts.

Jehovah warned their dad, Eli, who was serving as the high priest of Israel at the time (the same one who went on to mentor Samuel), about allowing his sons to be self-centered gluttons: "So why don't you respect the sacrifices and gifts? You honor your sons more than me. You grow fat on the best parts of the meat the Israelites bring to me" (1 Samuel 2:29 NCV). It's really interesting that the Hebrew word translated "honor" in this warning also means "to give weight to" or to "be weighty," which makes it a divine double entendre underscoring the fact that Eli and his boys were getting pudgy from all the marbled meat they were consuming! Obviously, part of the potluck methodology was to effect a healthy eating plan—essentially an other-worldly Weight Watchers—because when Eli and his sons bucked God's food rules, their cholesterol shot up, and they had to start buying their priestly garments at the Big and Tall Men's Shop. Ultimately, Hophni and Phinehas died young (on the same day, just as God had warned) as a result of their rebellious overeating, and poor old Eli got so fat and wobbly that he fell off a chair and broke his neck (1 Samuel 4:12–18 NCV).

The Creator of the universe pronounced judgment on Eli's family because they were more interested in stuffing themselves with rich food than they were with honoring and obeying Him. That is the very same reason Jesus made those seemingly harsh remarks in Luke 14. When He told the crowd they had to "hate" their families to be His disciples, Jesus was only emphasizing how they had to put Him first (the biblical idiom "to hate" actually means to "love less"). In other words, Christians have to make Christ our main course, not a side dish. The Bread of Life must become the biggest thing on our plate.

Hope for Our Ongoing Stories

My mom, who has the metabolism of a middle school boy and earned a lifelong membership to Weight Watchers because she's maintained her goal weight forever, has a magnet on her refrigerator that reads, "Nothing tastes as good as thin feels." And to be honest, I've always hated that magnet. Unlike Mom, I was in a chubby season for a very long time. Although I'm close to my goal weight now, I could easily puff back up. That's true mainly because I tend to misdiagnose the ache in my heart as rumbling in my stomach and shove more than I should in my mouth. I can totally imagine myself hustling for chocolate chip cookies outside the temple instead of going inside and letting God soothe the hunger in my soul. But I've decided I'll adopt her magnet motto, if I can change the word "thin" to the phrase "being loved by Jesus." *Nothing tastes as good as being loved by Jesus feels.* Now there's a slogan I'd plaster on my kitchen appliances and car bumper. That's a diet I can sink my teeth into!

Living in Light of His Story

Dear Jesus, I really am hungry for intimacy with You! I want to experience what David exclaims in Psalm 63:3–5: "Because your love is better than life, my lips will glorify you. I will praise you as long as I live, and in your name I will lift up my hands. I will be fully satisfied as with the richest of foods; with singing lips my mouth will praise you" (UPDATED NIV). Please help me crave Your presence more than anything or anyone else and be completely satisfied by Your spirit. Amen.

Personal Reflection and/or Group Discussion Questions

1. What are two or three running themes of the unhealthy thoughts that most often clog your heart and mind (e.g., weight, finances, relationships)?

2. How do you typically pig out (e.g., food, shopping sprees) when you're stressed out by the circumstances of your own life?

3. If you could choose just one particularly toxic thought or coping habit from which to fast, what would it be?

4. Read Proverbs 3:9–10. Using the context of heart and mind instead of finances, how would you paraphrase these two verses?

5. Describe a recent terrible-horrible-no-good-very-bad-day when you *didn't* "hustle for chocolate chip cookies outside the temple" and instead went immediately inside to let God soothe the hunger in your soul.

6. Read Psalm 63. What adjectives, illustrations, metaphors, or movie scenes best depict how intimacy with God satisfies your soul better than anything else?

Journal Entry

Please consider completing this sentence in your personal journal:

So, today I've been thinking about dropping a few pounds of _____, *Jesus, and . . .*

chapter 4
NO FANGS ALLOWED

*There is nothing more ugly than a Christian orthodoxy without
understanding or without compassion.*[1]

—Francis A. Schaeffer

So, today I've been thinking about dangerous things.

I actually started pondering these things earlier in the
week when I went for a hike with my friend Kelly. We met at
Radnor Lake State Park, and it was a perfect fall day. The
temperature was in the mid-60s, and the sky was robin's-
egg blue, which made the park feel even more like paradise.
Not that it needs any help, what with gaggles of Canadian
geese swimming on the water, cliques of curious deer graz-
ing mere feet away from the trails, and fabulous views of
hills ablaze in orange and yellow and red. We talked about

how beautiful Tennessee is and how thankful we were for cooler weather as we started our trek. Then we stopped just two hundred or so yards later to admire a long, skinny, chartreuse snake that was stretched across the trail sunning itself. I am not a fan of slithery things, but this little guy was obviously not the poisonous kind and was such a lovely, vibrant color. Plus, he looked so happy and lethargic soaking in the afternoon warmth, it was hard not to like him.

After a minute or two, I poked him with the tip of my running shoe so he'd scoot away into the safety of the forest and wouldn't get squished by some oblivious chunky guy in hiking boots (several of whom had already lumbered past without looking down). Then Kelly and I resumed hiking, arms pumping, and continued chatting about God and His glorious creation.

About thirty minutes later, when we were huffing up the steepest part of the trail, she called out with noticeable energy, "Lisa, there's another one!"

I turned around to see her pointing at a dead branch on the ground. I sighed inwardly and thought, *She's overdoing it a bit on this whole nature-lover thing*, but I didn't want to dampen her enthusiasm for the great outdoors. So I said, "Oh, wow." I stared at the big twig alongside her for five or ten seconds and hoped the fact that I thought her affection for felled wood was weird wasn't showing on my face. But then the "branch" moved and raised its scary, triangular head, and I realized I'd narrowly missed stepping on a copperhead!

I must admit that I shrieked a little and hopped up and down. Mind you, they were small hops. I did not succumb to full panic mode as the time I almost stepped on a snake *in my house*. Yes, you read correctly; there was a horrible, nasty reptile *in my house*.

It happened like this. It was late one Sunday afternoon last summer, and I was unloading luggage from a weekend trip. I'd just flopped my big suitcase on the bed when I thought, *I'd better go to the restroom before I go back out to the car or I'm going to bust a kidney.* Moments later, I was washing my hands and noticed movement out of the corner of my eye in the doorway between the bathroom and my bedroom. I glanced over and screamed bloody murder because there was a giant serpent (only a slight exaggeration), reared up, and striking at me. I backed up, still screaming, and quickly realized I was trapped in my own bathroom. The snake was not only raised up about two feet in the air and lunging at me, he was also blocking my exit.

I've been in several car accidents, have literally swum with sharks off the coast of Belize, and have to stand on a scale in the doctor's office at least once a year, yet never have I felt such sheer panic. I was breathing short, desperate breaths. I could feel the blood pounding in my ears. It felt as if a band was tightening around my chest.

I cried, "Jesus, help me!" aloud several times and tried to control my racing mind. But before I could calm down, the snake started slithering toward me, and so I sort of panicked and snatched a plunger from under the sink and started trying to joust him away. The nightmare became darker when he sank his fangs into the black rubber. I screamed again and slung his writhing body back to the doorway. While he lay there stunned, I jerked open the linen closet and grabbed the biggest beach towel I could find and threw it on top of him and vaulted over the wriggling pink wad like an Olympic hurdler.

Then I raced out of the house. I collapsed weakly on the back steps and pondered my next move. I thought, *I don't have a boyfriend or any male relatives living in Tennessee, and I don't think this merits a 911 call.* And like the idiot who opens the closet door where the ax-wielding lunatic is hiding in horror movies, I walked back into the house. When I got to my bedroom, I could see the shape of the snake still beneath the towel, so I found an old softball bat (which I've kept hidden in a corner closet for years just in case I needed it to whack an intruder) and began to pummel the towel. I figured my mahogany floors are supposed to look old anyway, and a few bat dings would only make their appearance more weathered.

After at least twenty hearty wallops, the lump stopped wiggling. Thinking the serpent had surely expired, I flipped up the edge of the towel with the handle of the bat and then fell back on my bottom when that beady-eyed monster jumped out and tried to bite me again! Suffice it to say, I was still pretty quivery an hour later after my contractor heroically captured the beast in a white bucket and chopped him in half with a shovel in the backyard.

Ken reasoned it had probably crawled up through the rock chimney from under the house to escape from the extreme summer temperatures and assured me it was not poisonous. Then he explained the reason it was so aggressive—I had unwittingly stepped on it with my platform shoes when I first entered the bathroom (I like high heels because of the elongating effect), as evidenced by the big, flat footprint on its back. He said the snake was just protecting itself from being stomped again or, worse still, plunged by a big, shrieking human.

However, I didn't feel bad about scaring that snake and didn't shed one tear during its dissection either. I don't like things with fangs anywhere near me.

Jesus encourages us to watch out for the snakes in our stories too.

Jesus and Dangerous Things

Jesus was born in the town of Bethlehem in Judea during the time when Herod was king. When Jesus was born, some wise men from the east came to Jerusalem. They asked, "Where is the baby who was born to be the king of the Jews? We saw his star in the east and have come to worship him."

When King Herod heard this, he was troubled, as well as all the people in Jerusalem. Herod called a meeting of all the leading priests and teachers of the law and asked them where the Christ would be born. They answered, "In the town of Bethlehem in Judea. The prophet wrote about this in the Scriptures: 'But you, Bethlehem, in the land of Judah, are important among the tribes of Judah. A ruler will come from you who will be like a shepherd for my people Israel.'"

Then Herod had a secret meeting with the wise men

and learned from them the exact time they first saw the star. He sent the wise men to Bethlehem, saying, "Look carefully for the child. When you find him, come tell me so I can worship him too."

After the wise men heard the king, they left. The star that they had seen in the east went before them until it stopped above the place where the child was. When the wise men saw the star, they were filled with joy. They came to the house where the child was and saw him with his mother, Mary, and they bowed down and worshiped him. They opened their gifts and gave him treasures of gold, frankincense, and myrrh. But God warned the wise men in a dream not to go back to Herod, so they returned to their own country by a different way. (Matthew 2:1–12 NCV)

The Heart of His Story

The birth narrative of Jesus is arguably the most beloved story of all time. Many of us have warm memories of hearing this passage read aloud during a candlelight Christmas Eve service or watching it depicted on stage during an Advent play, complete with little boys in bedazzled bathrobes acting out the parts of the wise men. People who don't even subscribe to the Christian faith appreciate this tale, and while they may question its veracity, they often still incorporate it into their holiday traditions. Along with eggnog, mistletoe, and Bing Crosby songs, the familiar characters of the Christmas story—Mary, Joseph, Baby Jesus, shepherds, and wise men—connect with a sweet, tender spot in our hearts.

But there are a few stinkers to beware of in this story too—a couple of snakes that were slithering through that nostalgic winter garden.

The viper with the loudest rattle is obviously Herod, the top dog of Judah. Herod was an ethnic Oreo; he was half-Jewish, therefore he was familiar with the Old Testament prophecies about Jesus, and he was half-Edomite, which was a tribe of people vehemently opposed to God and the coming Messiah. On top of his divided DNA, Herod was also infected with extreme anxiety. In fact, he was so paranoid about losing his power that he had his own wife and sons murdered to eradicate the possibility that they would usurp his throne. In light of his ruthless and suspicious nature, it's no wonder he was determined to kill the infant King the magi had come to worship. Herod was determined to destroy the Son of God.

The less poisonous-looking reptiles in this story are the leading priests and teachers of the law, the Sadducees and Pharisees. These two groups of religious leaders were usually on opposite sides of the fence. But in the case of Christ, they formed an equally hostile union. I can only imagine how frantic their behind-the-scenes negotiations were while they were waiting to address the king. I'm sure they haggled over who to appoint as their spokesperson and exactly how to answer Herod's question about the arrival of *Immanuel*, "God with us."

Evidently, they couldn't agree on a single representative, because Matthew reported that they gave a group response. "*They* answered: 'In the town of Bethlehem in Judea. The prophet wrote about this in the Scriptures: "But you, Bethlehem, in the land of Judah, are not just an insignificant village in Judah. A ruler will come from you who will be like a shepherd for my people Israel"'" (Matthew 2:5-6 NCV; emphasis added). I bet their beady eyes were darting around nervously the entire time they were reciting from Micah's prophecy, because they had knowingly left out the punch line—the part that would have made Herod hopping mad: "At that time the ruler of Israel will stand and take care of his people with the LORD's strength and with the power of the name of the LORD his God. The Israelites will live in safety, because his greatness will reach all over the earth" (Micah 5:4 NCV).

They cut and pasted God's Word because, just like egomaniacal Herod, they were scrambling to retain power, to protect their own best interests. They didn't want to give up their tenured positions and tax-exempt statuses. So, much like playground bullies grasping arms to form an unbreakable Red-Rover bond, the Pharisees and Sadducees formed an evil alliance to defeat the only begotten Son of God. They conspired against the very One who signed their paychecks. Even though they made a living by looking spiritual, these ancient Sunday school teachers had no real love for God or His people. Every time they opened their mouths, you could hear the audible hiss of deception.

Herod was out to *destroy*, and the religious leaders were out to *deceive*. Both behaviors are deadly. Both were active in trying to kill the "God with us" part of Christmas.

Hope for Our Ongoing Stories

I was visiting with a friend in her backyard last summer, enjoying sweet tea and casual conversation with her and her four-year-old daughter, Bella, when one of her rambunctious sons came racing up with a garter snake he had found lurking by the hydrangeas. He gleefully held the wriggling creature out toward his sister and proclaimed mischievously, "I got you a present!"

Bella coolly appraised the situation for a moment then replied confidently, "I do *not* want to play with him."

I've been praying for that same kind of discernment lately. I want to recognize the dangerous, potentially biting characters in my story: the people who create constant emotional debris with their destructive personalities or who refuse to shed the skin of deception, the ones who threaten the God-with-me peace in my life. I'm learning to keep my distance and to *pray for* snakes, but not make a habit of getting down in the dirt to *play with* them.

Living in Light of His Story

Dear Jesus, please give me the wisdom to tell the difference between broken people and biting people. Help me learn who to approach and who to avoid, to know when to step toward and when to step back. Amen.

Personal Reflection and/or Group Discussion Questions

1. Have the "snakes in your story" been mostly family members or not related to you?

2. With regard to the fight-or-flight theory, do you typically engage dangerous people head on or run like the wind the moment they bare their fangs?

3. What kind of venom—verbal, physical, emotional—has been the most painful for you in the past?

4. When it comes to slithery people, are you more wary of big biters like Herod or smaller, less obvious serpents like the Pharisees and Sadducees? Why?

5. Read Psalm 139:13–14 and Proverbs 4:23. How is our divine description in Psalm 139 related to the active command in Proverbs 4?

6. Read Luke 6:27–36 and 2 Corinthians 6:14–16. How would you describe the difference between loving your enemies/abusers and allowing yourself to become a victim of your enemies/abusers?

7. What are some tangible ways you've found to "turn the other cheek" when dealing with dangerous people without losing your whole head in the process?

Journal Entry

Please consider completing this sentence in your personal journal:

So, today I've been thinking about handling human snakes in a way that honors You, Jesus, and . . .

chapter 5
CAT APPRECIATION DAY

Listen to your life. See it for the fathomless mystery that it is. In the boredom and pain of it no less than in the excitement and gladness: touch, taste, smell your way to the holy and hidden heart of it because in the last analysis all moments are key moments, and life itself is grace.[1]

—Frederick Buechner

So, today I've been thinking about little, sweet things. Interestingly enough, the thought was prompted by a conversation about cats I had with my friend Karen, who's into all things feline and proudly showed me a picture on her cell phone of her three cats lounging on a windowsill. I had to bite my tongue to keep from telling her I didn't *like* cats. I come from a long line of people who are not into cats.

My grandmother wasn't a cat person; my mom isn't a cat person; and the apple didn't fall far from the tree because I, too, prefer the absolute—albeit codependent—devotion of dogs. But before the confession "I'm not really a cat person" tumbled from my lips, I remembered the tiny orange tabby who appeared on the rock wall outside my bedroom last summer and smiled.

Although I tried to shoo that baby cat away when he first materialized and make him slink back to wherever it was he came from, he stubbornly refused to leave my yard. To make matters much worse, a few days after my uninvited feline guest's arrival, I woke up at the crack of dawn to the sound of dogs barking. I stumbled to the window and rapped sharply on the glass, which usually causes my Jack Russell terriers to be quiet. Only this time their barking became louder and more frenzied. I muttered and grumbled to myself as I climbed out of bed and wriggled into a sweatshirt.

I opened the back door groggily and yelled, "Harley and Dottie, hush!" hoping my disheveled appearance would be enough to silence them and I wouldn't actually have to leave the comfort of the kitchen and traipse up the dewy hill for a face-to-snout reprimand. Then I noticed Dottie had something in her mouth and was furiously shaking it back and forth, and I began sprinting toward her yelling, "Dottie, no!" because even from a distance I recognized her new chew toy as the homeless kitty.

By the time I got there, Dottie had placed the slobbery ball of orange fur on the ground and was looking at me with the same shame-faced expression she wears when she's destroyed yet another dog bed. After shouting, "Bad, bad dog!" I scooped up the limp, barely breathing kitten and carried him into the house, thinking, *Every living thing deserves to have somebody with it when it dies*, and assuming I'd be burying the poor little thing within the hour.

Long story short, that plucky kitten miraculously recovered, so I christened him Lazarus. Within a week he was climbing trees and stalking butterflies and harassing me for fresh tuna. I couldn't help but spoil him, since I felt responsible for his near-death experience. More than once I found myself walking through the cat paraphernalia aisle at Target sheepishly piling things into my cart!

Lazarus even wormed his way into Harley's and Dottie's hearts and took to cuddling with them on chilly nights, purring away contently. Sometimes, when I watched him frolicking with them in the field behind my house, I was tempted to call out, "Lazarus, you idiot, those are the same mutts who tried to kill you!" But instead, I would just grin and think, *That silly cat has captivated us all.*

Almost a year from the day I met him, Lazarus wasn't at the back door waiting for his breakfast as usual, and I was immediately concerned. Much like the infamous orange Garfield that charmed millions from his perch in a comic strip, it wasn't like Lazarus to miss a meal. For the next several days, I went on long walks calling his name and even put up a "Lost Cat" sign in Puckett's, our local mom-and-pop grocery store. I kept hoping maybe he had simply gone on an extended hunt, as tomcats are prone to do.

Sadly, a week after he disappeared, a woman called

because she had noticed the sign and recognized Lazarus as the cat she had seen run over by the car in front of her when she was driving her kids to school. She carefully explained what she had witnessed and how he hadn't suffered, because he'd been killed instantly. I told her that I really appreciated her call and was glad to know definitively what had happened to him. Then I hung up the phone, sat down heavily on my bed, and cried.

I still miss Lazarus. When he died, it was almost as if I had lost my pinky toe—not something you tend to appreciate, yet its absence leaves you noticeably off balance. I find myself often glancing up at the crook in the tree where he used to lounge and feel my heart skip a beat when I see another tabby that resembles him. Grieving for that haughty critter has been a poignant reminder for me to be more appreciative of and attentive to all the little "kisses from God" that are woven into our lives.

I think intentional gratitude, especially for the small gifts that come wrapped in ordinary paper (or fur), is a necessary ingredient to living out an authentically joyful story. When we recognize that clean water, cold watermelon, red leaves in October, warm coats on cold days, and even a cat purring against one's legs are small demonstrations of our Redeemer's plan to bless mankind, it cements our hope and security. It anchors our prone-to-wander hearts to the truth of God's sovereign goodness and grace and to the fact that, regardless of what we're currently walking through, we can rest in His absolute affection.

Jesus provides sweet gifts every single day of our stories.

Jesus and Little, Sweet Things

When the eighth day arrived, the day of circumcision, the child was named Jesus, the name given by the angel before he was conceived.

Then when the days stipulated by Moses for purification were complete, they took him up to Jerusalem to offer him to God as commanded in God's Law: "Every male who opens the womb shall be a holy offering to God," and also to sacrifice the "pair of doves or two young pigeons" prescribed in God's Law.

In Jerusalem at the time, there was a man, Simeon by name, a good man, and a man who lived in the prayerful expectancy of help for Israel. And the Holy Spirit was on him. The Holy Spirit had shown him that he would see the Messiah of God before he died. Led by the Spirit, he entered the Temple. As the parents of the child Jesus brought him in to carry out the rituals of the Law, Simeon took him into his arms and blessed God: God, you can now release your servant; release me in peace as you promised. With my own eyes I've seen your salvation; it's now out in the open for everyone to see: A God-revealing light to the non-Jewish nations, and of glory for your people Israel.

Jesus' father and mother were speechless with surprise at these words. Simeon went on to bless them, and said to Mary his mother, This child marks both the failure and the recovery of many in Israel, a figure misunderstood and contradicted—the pain of a sword-thrust through you—but the rejection will force honesty, as God reveals who they really are.

Anna the prophetess was also there, a daughter of Phanuel from the tribe of Asher. She was by now a very old woman. She had been married seven years and a widow for eighty-four. She never left the Temple area, worshiping night and day with her fastings and prayers. At the very time Simeon was praying, she showed up, broke into an anthem of praise to God, and talked about the child to all who were waiting expectantly for the freeing of Jerusalem. (Luke 2:21–38 MSG)

The Heart of His Story

I think one of the sweetest gifts God gave during His Son's earthly ministry happened when Jesus was only eight days old. He bequeathed it to two people—a man named Simeon and a widow named Anna. Simeon's age isn't specified, but Bible scholars presume him to be elderly, in light of the phrase, "The Holy Spirit had shown him that he would see the Messiah of God before he died," which would be a weird biblical footnote if he had been a young man. Also, his "Okay, I can die happy now" response after meeting the Christ child—"God, you can now release your servant; release me in peace as you promised"—implies his advanced age. Anna is verifiably old because, if you do the math, she was married for seven years and had been a widow for eighty-four. So, assuming she married around fourteen, as most good Jewish girls at the time did, she was at least 105!

Luke explains that both of these elderly people hung out at the temple a lot because of their devotion to God. But given their AARP status, I can't help wondering if they were a little lonely as well. They probably didn't have anyone to go home to. No one to talk to at the dinner table. No one to sit on the couch with and watch *Hebrew Idol*. Nothing in their tidy apartments at the City of God Retirement Center to keep them company but a tabby cat and cataracts. So they puttered around the church every day, praying at the altar, hobbling back and forth on errands for the priests, carrying boxes of candles up from the basement, and carefully rubbing each pew with linseed oil until it gleamed. Temple regulars grew accustomed to always seeing the white-haired gentleman wearing high-water khakis and the nice old lady who smelled like Pledge. Most worshippers didn't give Simeon and Anna any more thought than they did the shiny pews or the plentiful supply of candles up front.

But then one day a teenage couple walked in the front door of the temple. The young husband was wearing tattered but clean jeans and seemed to have birds squawking in his backpack. While his wife—she couldn't have been more than fifteen—was carrying what looked to be a brand-new baby. They shyly approached Simeon and the young man cleared his throat and said, "I'm sorry to bother you, sir, but can you tell us where to go to give God an offering on behalf of our little boy?"

Simeon put down his mop and took a deep breath to steady himself. Then he reached his gnarled hands toward the new mom and asked gently, "May I hold Him?"

Mary nodded and handed the newborn Son of God to Simeon. He cradled the pink-cheeked Messiah for several minutes and then began to sing a praise chorus he made up years before but had never actually sung out loud.

Anna, who had been in the women's restroom the whole time, refilling the paper towel dispenser, shuffled back toward the sanctuary when she heard Simeon's baritone voice warbling, thinking, *What's that old goose up to now?* His voice rose in pitch as she wobbled her way there, causing her feeble heart to skip a beat. She didn't know Simeon was singing; she was afraid he had fallen down and broken his hip again, until she turned the corner and saw her dear old friend's enraptured countenance. Then she saw the baby in his arms and, realizing immediately the miracle that was taking place, she ran toward him with the speed and agility of a girl!

Hope for Our Ongoing Stories

Day after day, year after year, Anna and Simeon accepted and appreciated the diminutive joys that came their way. Someplace to go to volunteer and feel useful. A friend with whom to share their umbrellas and their prayer requests. Free WiFi in the temple lobby. I can't help wondering if their willingness to recognize the sweet, little gifts Jehovah blesses us with each and every day is part of why He chose them to be recipients of the same incomparable surprise present He gave the shepherds wandering in their fields by night. Good news and great joy—the Savior of the world wrapped in an ordinary blanket.

Living in Light of His Story

Dear Jesus, forgive me when I'm so greedy about big gifts that I overlook all the small ones. Thank You for the heat that's coursing through my house right now on this cold night. Thank You that there's milk that hasn't expired yet in the refrigerator. Thank You for the clean sheets that will greet me when I go to bed. Thank You for giving me life and breath and keeping me in Your perfect care for one more day. Amen.

Personal Reflection and/or Group Discussion Questions

1. What are the first five things that come to your mind for which you want to thank God?

2. What are you thankful for that took place today?

3. Read James 1:17. Wherever you are—gathered around a table with your small group or sitting in the bathtub (one of my favorite places to read)—take thirty seconds to inventory everything around you for which you're thankful.

4. Who in your life most resembles Anna or Simeon—someone who receives even the most diminutive gifts from God with obvious gratitude?

5. For what little gift have you waited the longest (e.g., a haircut or dental crown during tough financial times)?

6. Read 2 Peter 3:9. What is it about waiting for a gift that makes it more precious when we finally receive it?

Journal Entry

Please consider completing this sentence in your personal journal:

So, today I've been thinking about the infinite list of little gifts with which You've blessed me, Jesus, and . . .

part 2
REAL GIFTS

chapter 6
JOHNNY COME LATELY

*God is asking me, the unworthy, to forget my unworthiness and that
of my brothers, and dare to advance in the love which has redeemed
and renewed us all in God's likeness. And to laugh, after all, at the
preposterous ideas of "worthiness."*[1]

—Thomas Merton

So, today I've been thinking about two things: about
the gift of fathers and the gift of forgiveness.

It took me longer than most to trust in the perfect
Fatherhood of God—to feel comfortable with the Alpha and
Omega as Abba. It wasn't difficult to consider God as our
Creator-Redeemer, but I secretly imagined Him to be a
pretty distant dad. My misconception was due largely to my
parents' divorce when I was five. Watching my own dad walk

away to another woman and child left me a bit wary of father figures. He did the best he could to love me well on weekends, but distrust had already wormed its way into my heart. And it was wedged firmly in place over the next several years by a few men who came and went from our lives and did things to me that men shouldn't do to grown women, much less little girls.

Then mom married John Angel, a broad-shouldered man with twinkling blue eyes, who was well respected in our community because of his past history as a football star and then-current position as the superintendent of schools. At first, I thought "Dad Angel" was the greatest man in the world and was determined to make him proud of me. I can still remember his striding into our school cafeteria one day soon after he had become my stepfather. Although he entered the room with two or three other men, it was obvious he was the most important one in the posse because of how our principal and teachers deferred to him. My chest swelled with pride when he walked purposefully over to where I was sitting on his way out. While I'm sure I turned ten shades of red when he tousled my hair and asked if I was having a good day, inwardly I was beaming!

However, it became apparent very quickly that there was a big difference between Dad Angel's charming public persona and the authoritarian chauvinist who moved into our house. The scowling guy who monitored my eating habits because he didn't approve of heavyset females was a far cry from the affable leader who strolled through Southside Elementary. The passage of time and a Porsche's worth of dollars spent in professional counseling have helped me understand that most of the welts he inflicted on my heart were unintentional. His lack of love for me was due mostly to the anemic affection he received as a child. And that, much like a male peacock's fancy bottom, his misogyny and machismo were probably just elaborate camouflage for his own fears and feelings of inadequacy.

What I never came to terms with was his spiritual condition. His stony heart toward God bothered me far more than his bigotry or bad words. More than twenty years ago, in 1989, I wrote in the front of my Bible, "Dear God, please keep my heart stirred until Dad Angel comes to faith in You." Needless to say, when I got a call last September telling me he had suffered two strokes and might not make it through the night, I was anxious. Knowing I couldn't get to his bedside until the next day, I prayed desperately, "Please don't let him die, Lord! Not yet, not until he makes peace with You."

By the grace of a Creator he had refused to acknowledge, Dad Angel pulled through, and two nights after he came home from the hospital, I got to experience an even greater miracle. We were nibbling on cheese toast, and I started talking—for what seemed like the millionth time—about how much God loves us. To my surprise, he listened and nodded appreciatively, instead of snorting in disgust or getting up from the table and walking away as he always had in the past. Then he nonchalantly said something positive about God. I tried not to gasp and wondered if he was lucid. (He was diagnosed with Alzheimer's disease a few years ago and sometimes is "all there" mentally but sometimes isn't.) When I realized he was completely coherent, I asked gently when his beliefs had changed.

He answered candidly, "The closer you get to the grave, the more interested you get in God."

Later that night, I asked if he would read the Bible aloud to me. He gruffly asked why, so I explained that it was my favorite Book, and his was one of my favorite voices. It was all I could do not to squeal with glee when he agreed. He sat down in his favorite recliner and slowly opened a big King James Bible. In the forty years since Dad Angel and Mom got married, I had never seen or heard him read Scripture. I can't remember a time when he said *God* without following it up with a curse word. Yet here he was carefully turning the thin pages of Mom's old Bible. I felt like pinching myself, because it was as if I was watching a scene from the way I had dreamed our family could be.

I reached over, flipped to the middle of the gospel of John, and asked, "Dad, will you please start reading right here?" thinking, *If this is the only time I ever hear him read the Bible, I want to hear him repeat what Jesus said: "I am the way, the truth, and the life. No one comes to the Father except through me"* (John 14:6). Not that I have control issues or anything!

He put his gnarled eighty-seven-year-old finger at the top of the page, started reading, and read through to the very end of John's gospel account. He read aloud from chapter 14 through chapter 21. Through Gethsemane and Golgotha and the empty tomb. The only time he stopped was when I interrupted him after he recited the story of how Thomas believed after touching the nail wounds in our Savior's resurrected hands in chapter 20.

I said, "Dad, do you believe in Jesus?"

He looked up at me from the text with raised brows and said, "What?"

I pressed on slowly. "Well, Thomas was so analytical that he had to experience a tangible Jesus to believe. And you're really analytical like Thomas but haven't gotten to experience Jesus in the flesh. You've never touched His hands. Do you still believe?"

Dad paused for a while; he seemed to be sizing up whether my question was worth answering. After several long seconds, with just a hint of irritation, he said, "Yes," and resumed reading.

I don't have adequate words to describe how grateful and overwhelmed I am that God softened my stepfather's heart, that He allowed me to share a few tender moments with him at the end of his life, and that, because of Christ's tenacious compassion, I might get to have a real relationship with Dad Angel in glory. It's been the sweetest answer to a prayer I had all but stopped praying.

Our Redeemer's gift of forgiveness means even the most difficult characters in our stories can be reconciled into a right relationship with God the Father.

JESUS AND THE GIFT OF FORGIVENESS

"For the kingdom of heaven is like a master of a house who went out early in the morning to hire laborers for his vineyard. After agreeing with the laborers for a denarius a day, he sent them into his vineyard. And going out about the third hour he saw others standing idle in the marketplace, and to them he said, 'You go into the vineyard too, and whatever is right I will give you.' So they went. Going out again about the sixth hour and the ninth hour, he did the same. And about the eleventh hour he went out and found others standing. And he said to them, 'Why do you stand here idle all day?' They said to him, 'Because no one has hired us.' He said to them, 'You go into the vineyard too.' And when evening came, the owner of the vineyard said to his foreman, 'Call the laborers and pay them their wages, beginning with the last, up to the first.' And when those hired about the eleventh hour came, each of them received a denarius. Now when those hired first came, they thought they would receive more, but each of them also received a denarius. And on receiving it they grumbled at the master of the house, saying, 'These last worked only one hour, and you have made them equal to us who have borne the burden of the day and the scorching heat.' But he replied to one of them, 'Friend, I am doing you no wrong. Did you not agree with me for a denarius? Take what belongs to you and go. I choose to give to this last worker as I give to you. Am I not allowed to do what I choose with what belongs to me? Or do you begrudge my generosity?' So the last will be first, and the first last." (Matthew 20:1–16 ESV)

The Heart of His Story

Jesus often told stories, or *parables*, to people who gathered to hear Him teach. Keeping in mind that most of the crowd was illiterate (very few people had formal educations during the time of Christ), the Good Shepherd guided them with lessons they could relate to, instead of esoteric observations about Mosaic Law. But the stories He told didn't resemble the silly, innocuous tales in some children's books. They were more like a velvet sword or riddles with teeth. Some people listened to His parables, understood, and moved closer toward Jesus in belief. Others listened to His parables, didn't understand, and walked away shaking their heads in unbelief. That might have been the case when Jesus told this perplexing story, except for the fact that He was only talking to His disciples here. Peter, James, John, Andrew, Philip, Bartholomew, Matthew, Thomas, James the son of Alphaeus, Thaddaeus, Simon the Zealot, and Judas were the only ones listening.

At first glance, the Twelve were probably thinking the vineyard owner seemed a bit disorganized, if not completely irrational. I can picture Pete scratching his head, thinking, *What sane businessman would hire three different groups of workers at three different times on the same day and pay those who only worked a little while a full day's wage? How'd he make a profit? How'd he even stay in business? Good night, his behavior is plum nutty! I mean, had thousands of bunches of ripe grapes suddenly appeared that he hadn't noticed on previous strolls through his vineyard? Was he having marital troubles that clouded his mind at work? Did a barista accidentally put five extra shots of espresso into his morning latte?* Given the fact that the disciples were familiar with the way Jesus structured His parables by now and would have immediately recognized that the master in the story represented the Master of the universe, the other eleven were likely scratching their heads too!

But when we take the time to ponder it, this particular parable is tailor-made for followers of Christ. While many of us know Paul's explanation of salvation by heart—"For it is by grace you have been saved, through faith—and this is not from yourselves, it is the gift of God" (Ephesians 2:8)—most of us still water the plant of self-righteousness on the windowsill of our hearts. We may be thinking to ourselves that we're spiritually cleaner than the chick who smells like cigarette smoke in our Beth Moore Bible study. We may be assuming that our regular church attendance is adding up like divine frequent-flyer miles. Or we may secretly believe that we somehow *deserve* God's acceptance and approval more than the stinkers we rub shoulders with on a regular basis.

That makes the question, "Do you begrudge?" the master posed to the fussy workers, who thought they deserved a bonus for working all day long instead of just for the last sixty minutes, especially convicting. And it sliced even deeper in the language Jesus was speaking at the time, "Is your eye evil?" Yikes! Mine often is. I tend to see myself as more "forgiveness worthy" than people like my stepdad. I've made a habit of stroking and feeding an inner pet idol of *deservedness*. Sometimes I even buy little sweaters for it.

Late, great pastor Dr. James Montgomery Boice authored a book explaining the parables of Christ that has really helped me understand and apply them. And one of my favorite explanations is what he wrote about the last men hired by the orchard master:

Apparently they had been willing to work, were eager to work, and undoubtedly needed it. But they had not been hired. We are to think that the owner hired them not for what he could get out of them in just a few hours, but because they needed the work, and that he paid them the full denarius for the same reason. The owner was not thinking of profit. He was thinking of people, and he was using his abundant means to help them.[2]

Those marvelous lines have been working like liquid antifreeze in the water dish of my nasty pet named "I deserve"!

Hope for Our Ongoing Stories

One of my dear friends had a daddy who was so mean she actually prayed for God to go ahead and take him out, if He wasn't planning on saving him. Of course, she was wholly undone when her father walked an aisle and gave his crooked heart to Jesus at the age of eighty-four! People. Messy people. Mistake-prone people. Even mean, old daddies. God loves them all. It is His will that none of us should perish. And He goes to extravagant lengths to accomplish His will.

May I end this chapter with a suggestion from one stinker to another? Make a short list of the people in your life story who appear to be the least deserving of God's forgiveness. Pray for them by name—that they will stumble into the redemptive grace of Jesus Christ—at least once a week. And for goodness' sake, instead of praying for God to take them out if He's not going to save them, ask Him to kill the idol of deservedness in your own heart!

Living in Light of His Story

Dear Jesus, I'm so humbled and convicted and glad You don't give me what I deserve. Instead of taking me out, You take me into Your loving arms. Please forgive me for smugly thinking I deserve more grace than the other sinners in my story. And help me to see them in the light of how precious they are to You, even on their worst days. Amen.

Personal Reflection and/or Group Discussion Questions

1. Are you more comfortable with the concept of God as the Creator of the universe or as your heavenly Father? Explain.

2. Would you be more likely to kneel before God in obeisance or crawl up into the safety of His lap?

3. What do you think are the top three or four attributes of a good dad?

4. How would you describe the "idol of deservedness"? How does it typically rear its ugly head in your life?

5. Read Ephesians 2:8–9. How would you explain the basic message of these verses to a child? How would you condense it into a three- or four-word book or movie title?

6. If you feel comfortable doing so, describe the character in your life story whom you'd vote as the "least likely to come to faith in Christ."

7. Read Romans 12:17–21. Mark Twain wrote, "Forgiveness is the fragrance the violet sheds on the heel that has crushed it." In light of his poignant metaphor, on whose heel have you left the most perfume? Whose perfume has wafted from your heel?

Journal Entry

Please consider completing this sentence in your personal journal:

So, today I've been thinking about the lavish gift of forgiveness You extend to sinners of all shapes and sizes, Jesus, and . . .

chapter 7
GETTING OUR SQUEEZE ON

God's arms are always extended; we are the ones who turn away.[1]
—Philip Yancey

So, today I've been thinking about the gift of touch.

It is probably because it's a cold morning, and I'm sitting here by the fireplace, wishing someone else were sitting here with me rubbing my freezing feet. My heart warms up at the mere thought of physical touch. It makes me happy to hold the hand of someone I love or hug someone I like or scoot up next to a friend and drape an arm across her shoulders when we're praying together. There's just something about physical affection that sweetens the bond of relationship. It's kind of like the sugar and cream I liberally splash in my coffee—I think they enhance the flavor of something that was already pretty good. Of course, some java addicts prefer their coffee black. They actually think it tastes better without the added calories. And there are certainly those who prefer their relationships without touch too—who think life should be a noncontact sport.

One of them used to attend a Bible study I taught in Nashville. (For the sake of her anonymity, I won't use her real name. But for the sake of amusement, I'll call her "Fridgeeta.") The attendance in this particular Bible study usually hovered around sixty or so women, and we got together every week for several hours for five years. That meant we shared a whole lot of life together. We walked through marriages and births and miscarriages and divorces. Sometimes we laughed until tears streamed down our faces and sometimes we cried until it seemed we didn't have any tears left. We became very authentic and comfortable with each other, a pretty close-knit kind of family.

Therefore, a year or so into this girlfriends-who-love-God journey, I thought it would be a good idea to begin each session by standing up as a group and turning in one direction and rubbing the shoulders of whoever happened to be sitting beside us that morning. I thought a brief, communal massage could help get out the kinks of stress and distraction before we sat back down and tried to focus on God's Word and how it applied to our sometimes difficult lives. Judging by the oohs and aahs and exclamations of "rub a little more to the left" in the room, it worked. Well, it worked for everybody except Fridgeeta, who harrumphed her way through the rubbing routine and ultimately began showing up ten or fifteen minutes late so she could avoid it altogether. Soon enough, she made an appointment with me to officially express her disapproval.

I can still remember the way she sat down with a bit of a huff in my office, then crossed her arms and pursed her lips before launching into why she thought it was completely inappropriate for grown women to "grope" each other. She went on to complain that she wasn't a demonstrative person and didn't feel comfortable having other people squeeze her shoulders, especially in church. She finished with an indignant flourish, saying, "If I want a massage, I'll make an appointment with a professional and pay for it!"

Although I tend to speak first and think later, I found myself pausing for several long moments before responding. What I really wanted to do was gather her walled-off little self into a bear hug and squeeze until she stopped squirming. Instead, I said, "Maybe it would help if I explained the method behind what comes across as madness to you." I told Fridge that I meet women on a weekly basis who receive very little, if any, healthy physical touch. Some of the manicured, perfectly coiffed women who occupy pews every Sunday in our congregation have been victims of physical abuse by their husbands or sexual abuse by someone they knew when they were growing up. For most of us, rubbing a friend's shoulders is no big deal, not even a blip on our daily radar. However, for a woman whose private experience with physicality has been a closed fist or an unwanted violation, having someone safe touch her with a hand that means her well can be deeply comforting. Even healing, like offering a sip of cool water to someone who's dying of thirst in the desert.

Furthermore, I told Fridgie, "God wired us for touch." Medical studies have proven that physical touch boosts our immune systems, improves our psychological states, and can literally save lives. Historical documents reveal a crude and cruel thirteenth-century study in which Frederick II, the reigning German emperor, wondered what language children would speak if they were never spoken to. So he selected several newborns in an orphanage and instructed nurses to feed them, but not to talk to them or touch them. Every single one of those babies died. Dr. Fritz Talbot conducted a more scientific study regarding the effects of touch on babies in the 1940s and established a conclusive connection between touch and an infant's ability to thrive. Additional data gathered from orphanages proves a distinct correlation between holding, cuddling with, and carrying infants, and their survival rates. Obviously, from the moment we're first plopped on this spinning orb called Earth, we need a loving, literal connection with someone else who's wearing a suit of skin too.

I concluded my defense by carefully explaining that the Gospels describe Jesus Himself as a toucher. There are multiple cases in which our Savior reached out and embraced people when a simple nod or quick handshake would have sufficed. He intentionally used tactile methods—hugging a leper, placing His hands on a crippled woman's spine—in most of His healing miracles. When the disciples tried to keep little children from interacting with Jesus (like most kids, they probably had sticky hands and dirty knees and, therefore, the disciples thought they were too messy to interact with the Messiah), the Lamb of God beckoned them to pile onto His lap (Mark 10:13–16). And the defining moment of the apostle John's life was when Jesus allowed him to lean back against His chest during the last meal they shared together (John 21:20). In short, I told my skittish friend, our Savior was a master masseur.

The following week, Fridgeeta sheepishly showed up on time and submitted to being loved on. It took months for her to loosen up, but eventually she got to where she'd almost purr if you rubbed her shoulders in just the right spot!

Our Redeemer's gift of touch provides healing connection and can warm even the coldest heart.

JESUS AND THE GIFT OF TOUCH

Walking down the street, Jesus saw a man blind from birth. His disciples asked, "Rabbi, who sinned: this man or his parents, causing him to be born blind?" Jesus said, "You're asking the wrong question. You're looking for someone to blame. There is no such cause-effect here. Look instead for what God can do. We need to be energetically at work for the One who sent me here, working while the sun shines. When night falls, the workday is over. For as long as I am in the world, there is plenty of light. I am the world's Light."

He said this and then spit in the dust, made a clay paste with the saliva, rubbed the paste on the blind man's eyes, and said, "Go, wash at the Pool of Siloam" (Siloam means "Sent"). The man went and washed—and saw.

Soon the town was buzzing. His relatives and those who year after year had seen him as a blind man begging were saying, "Why, isn't this the man we knew, who sat here and begged?"

Others said, "It's him all right!" But others objected, "It's not the same man at all. It just looks like him."

He said, "It's me, the very one." They said, "How did your eyes get opened?"

"A man named Jesus made a paste and rubbed it on my eyes and told me, 'Go to Siloam and wash.' I did what he said. When I washed, I saw." (John 9:1–11 MSG)

The Heart of His Story

In traditional Middle Eastern culture, beggars—especially those who are physically handicapped as this blind man was—are recognized as an unavoidable part of community life. And during the time of Christ, beggars congregated wherever there was a lot of foot traffic; say, outside the temple or the city gates, and they typically proclaimed something along the lines of, "Give to God!" loudly to the people passing by.

In light of the general understanding that God expected "regular folks" to help those who were less fortunate, beggars were essentially saying, "My needs are beside the point. I am offering you a golden opportunity to fulfill one of your obligations to the Creator of the universe. Furthermore, this is a public place, and if you give to me here, you will gain a reputation as an honorable, compassionate, pious person."

When anyone caved to their manipulative tactics and handed over a coin or two, they would jump to their feet and proclaim the giver to be the most noble person they'd ever met and invoke God's blessing on the giver, his family, his friends, his associates, his going out and coming in.[2] It was a very effective accost-with-guilt-and-then-heap-with-effusive-praise strategy that ensured most beggars enough alms to scrape by day to day.

Of course, while those traipsing to and from their nine-to-five jobs at cubicles in downtown Jerusalem were *used* to the presence of beggars, they didn't necessarily *like* them. I mean, here they were dutifully fulfilling their responsibilities: paying their own bills and taxes, already stretching their paychecks so as to cover extras, such as their kids' karate lessons and their intrusive mother-in-law's meds. The last thing they needed was another grimy paw trying to get into their wallets and pilfer from their meager stashes. My guess is that more than a few commuters rolled their eyes and sighed irritably, even as they dropped fifty cents into the outstretched palm or cup of a beggar.

Adding to the disregard the general populace had toward beggars was the theological notion that infirmity was some sort of divine retribution, which is why the disciples asked Jesus, "Who sinned: this blind dude or his parents?" (John 9:1). Much as Job's friends had assumed centuries before, the disciples thought the beggar's physical handicap must be due to a moral deficiency. Surely he had done something horrible to deserve his stumbling lot in life. Christ's closest companions noticed the blind man's white-tipped cane and his Ray Charles glasses, but they didn't *see him*.

Jesus did. He looked past the dark shades and saw the hopelessness in the man's eyes. He recognized how lonely it was for him to live in a world of black—never being able to watch the first rays of the sun race through early morning mist; never having the thrill of distinguishing a dolphin fin from a wave as it breaks the cerulean surface of the ocean; never being able to experience the enraptured wonder of children's faces when they encounter things like snow or horses or Christmas trees for the first time. So the Son of God didn't reach into His pocket and pull out a crumbled dollar bill for this man; instead, He reached down and grabbed a handful of the earth He'd created and made a poultice of mud and saliva, then gently applied it to his sightless eyes. Jesus didn't just acknowledge the man's infirmity and toss a dismissive healing phrase into his cup of affliction; He *touched* the man with deep concern and tangible compassion, restoring both his eyesight and his heart in the process.

Hope for Our Ongoing Stories

I dated a professional football player for a very brief period of time, and the two most significant moments during the blip of our romantic relationship were when I realized his thigh was the same circumference as my waist, which made me feel unusually petite, and when he engaged a homeless man while we were walking to a restaurant one night in downtown Atlanta. We'd already observed the homeless man aggressively approach several other people and ask for money, so when Bruce stopped and said, "Hey man, what's your name?" I assumed he was going to give the guy a lecture about accosting innocent strangers. Instead, Bruce invited him to join us for dinner. He gestured to me and said, "This is my date, Lisa. Lisa, this is Howard." Then he grabbed me by the hand and Howard by the elbow and steered us both across the street to eat.

That colorful dinner date happened more than fifteen years ago, and I can only remember a few blurry details from Howard's story. I remember he described having to fight overseas while he served in the US military, although I can't recall which war or in what branch of service he served. And I remember his telling us how cold Atlanta could be in the wintertime if you were sleeping outside, but I don't recall if he was originally from the South or had moved there as an adult.

What I do remember clearly is the way Howard's face lit up every time Bruce clapped him on the back and made a comment like, "Wow, buddy, you've had so many adventures!" or "Gosh, I can't imagine how tough you've got to be to sleep on a steel grate—I don't think I'm man enough to do it!" I also remember talking at length about the love of God (Howard told us he was a Christian), as well as the way he hugged us after we said a prayer before going our separate ways. His physical vigor was obviously restored by that cheeseburger and fries, and I believe his emotional vigor was partly restored by the encounter too. By simply whacking him with manly affection, it's as if Bruce forced Howard's lifeblood of hope to start pumping again.

Jesus modeled the restorative effects of touch two thousand years ago. He typically used His *hands* to *heal*. Don't you think it behooves us as His disciples to keep the squeeze on?

Living in Light of His Story

Dear Jesus, thank You for truly seeing me and for always engaging me and never dismissing me. I look forward to the day when I get to actually see You face-to-Face in glory. I look forward to the day I get to literally feel Your holy arms around me. Amen.

Personal Reflection and/or Group Discussion Questions

1. On the scale of one to ten below in regard to being comfortable with physical affection—with one being "frosty" and ten being "hugging helpful salespeople at the mall"—circle the number that represents where you would place yourself.

   1   2   3   4   5   6   7   8   9   10

2. What is your favorite (nonsexual) form of physical affection?

3. How often would you guess you get healthy physical affection (e.g., a hug or holding hands during prayer) on a weekly basis?

4. How often do you think you need to receive healthy physical affection on a weekly basis?

5. Who gets the lion's share of your hugs?

6. Read John 21:20. When was the last time, figuratively speaking, that you leaned into the embrace of Jesus?

7. How did the conclusion of this chapter—"Jesus modeled the restorative effects of touch two thousand years ago. He typically used His *hands* to *heal*. Don't you think it behooves us as His disciples to keep the squeeze on?"—resonate with you? Were you encouraged, skeptical, or convicted? Please explain your answer.

Journal Entry

Please consider completing this sentence in your personal journal:

So, today I've been thinking about the gift You modeled for us of physical affection, Jesus, and . . .

chapter 8
THE BRIDE WHO TRIPPED DOWN THE AISLE

I think we understand on some level that control is illusory. It does not exist, particularly in the areas of hormones and hair.[1]

—Anita Renfroe

So, today I've been thinking about the gift of good humor.

It all started when my friends Chance and Jennifer told a story that made me laugh so hard my cheeks cramped! They've recently moved into a Pleasantville-like planned community filled with row after row of pretty homes with petite, albeit perfectly manicured, lawns. According to the developer's advertisements, the small lot size encourages interaction between neighbors, as do the proliferation of sidewalks, shared "open spaces," and a front porch requirement for every home in "Happyville." It's a wonderful concept for extreme extroverts; for people who find that mingling with neighbors helps them unwind after a long day at work; or for network marketing specialists, who are always looking for new contacts to whom they can pitch candles, vitamins, home goods, and jewelry.

But Chance and Jennifer are a pretty low-key, normal couple with two little girls, who share lots of close relationships with people from their church and the music business, so they don't feel the need (or have the time) for constant socialization with the other inhabitants of Happyville. However, after several neighbors made pointed comments about their lack of participation in block parties and barbecues, they started to feel guilty. Therefore, one Sunday afternoon, when Chance noticed a ton of cars parked outside a house on their street, he turned to Jennifer and said, "It looks like they're having one of those football-watching parties at the Smiths' again. I hate to even suggest this, but do you think we should go over there for a little while?"

Jennifer sighed and replied, "Maybe we should at least make an appearance, because I think we're getting the reputation of being antisocial." So they changed out of their baby-food-stained sweats and into presentable jeans. Then Chance grabbed a six-pack of beer from the pantry (they don't drink beer, but someone had given it to them as a welcome gift when they moved in), thinking they should take some kind of offering and that surely one of the rowdy Tennessee Titans fans would appreciate it. He and Jen strolled hand in hand down to the soiree, neither too enthused about it, but looking forward to getting the anti-social monkey off their backs.

Since the jovial host of the gathering had often bragged about his casual, open-door policy, Chance chose not to knock when they arrived and simply swung open the front door. He said they were a little taken aback by the sight of thirty people sitting around multiple tables eating real food, instead of ten or twelve gathered around a big-screen TV eating popcorn, especially when everyone looked up and eyed them curiously. Thinking the sit-down meal was some kind of fancy tailgate party, Chance held up the six-pack and announced with false cheer, "We're finally here!" He and Jen were further confused by the awkward silence that followed.

But nothing prepared them for what happened next when a very sober woman pulled them aside and asked who they were and what they were doing. Flustered by her less-than-warm greeting, they stammered out that they had come to join in the neighborhood football-watching fes-tivities. Her eyebrows shot up and Chance and Jen said they wanted to crawl in a hole when she went on to icily explain they were not only at the wrong house, but they were intrud-ing on a private meal after a funeral service!

After my guffaws subsided and I could speak again, I told Chance and Jen that their covered-dish disaster made me love them more than ever before! Then I confessed to being a member of the buffoon tribe too, because I have a list of embarrassing moments a mile long. They said I had to prove it by sharing one, so in honor of stumbling saints the world over, I described my most recent calamity.

A few days previously I'd gone to the BMW dealership, because the Check Engine light had appeared ominously on my instrument panel. I always feel like a bit of an imposter when I visit the dealership, because I got a good deal on a used SUV and don't really fit the luxury-car demographic. As a matter of fact, the salesmen usually give me the cold shoulder. I guess the fact that I'm typically wearing a ball cap with a ponytail hanging out the back and there are mulch remnants in the back of my car are dead giveaways that I can't afford a new BMW! But on this particular visit I was feeling more like a stereotypical expensive German car owner because I'd come from a business meeting and was wearing a dressy skirt with high heels.

I smiled at the attendant, who gallantly swooped in to open the car door for me when I pulled into the spotless "driver drop-off zone." For a brief moment, I felt wealthy and elegant, as if I were stepping from a limousine onto the red carpet. But the second my left heel hit the polished cement, it shot out from under me like a cartoon character stepping on a banana peel. Of course, my right leg stayed put in the car, so I ended up doing a painful split between the two. Then, because the floor was so slick, I got stuck. I couldn't get any leverage to pull myself upright. At that moment, I was seized by a charley horse— a truly excruciating cramp. Trust me when I tell you that a wincing, squealing woman rolling around on the floor of a BMW dealership with her skirt hiked up around her not-altogether-tiny waist attracts unwanted attention!

I'm so glad God created laughter and people to share it with. I love hanging out with friends like Chance and Jen, who don't take themselves too seriously and will giggle about their own gaffes! I'm even more grateful we're completely accepted by a divine Prince, who puts up with our bumbling nature, who thinks we're beautiful even when our feet are too swollen for glass slippers, and who surely winks affectionately when we've got pumpkin seeds stuck in our hair.

Our Redeemer's gift of good humor means that our bobbles and blunders won't ever disqualify us from His team!

JESUS AND THE GIFT OF GOOD HUMOR

Later, Jesus showed himself to his followers again—this time at Lake Galilee. This is how he showed himself: Some of the followers were together: Simon Peter, Thomas (called Didymus), Nathanael from Cana in Galilee, the two sons of Zebedee, and two other followers. Simon Peter said, "I am going out to fish."

The others said, "We will go with you." So they went out and got into the boat. They fished that night but caught nothing.

Early the next morning Jesus stood on the shore, but the followers did not know it was Jesus. Then he said to them, "Friends, did you catch any fish?"

They answered, "No."

He said, "Throw your net on the right side of the boat, and you will find some." So they did, and they caught so many fish they could not pull the net back into the boat.

The follower whom Jesus loved said to Peter, "It is the Lord!" When Peter heard him say this, he wrapped his coat around himself. (Peter had taken his clothes off.) Then he jumped into the water. The other followers went to shore in the boat, dragging the net full of fish. They were not very far from shore, only about a hundred yards. When the followers stepped out of the boat and onto the shore, they saw a fire of hot coals. There were fish on the fire, and there was bread.

Then Jesus said, "Bring some of the fish you just caught."

Simon Peter went into the boat and pulled the net to the shore. It was full of big fish, one hundred fifty-three in all, but even though there were so many, the net did not tear. Jesus said to them, "Come and eat." None of the followers dared ask him, "Who are you?" because they knew it was the Lord. Jesus came and took the bread and gave it to them, along with the fish.

This was now the third time Jesus showed himself to his followers after he was raised from the dead.

When they finished eating, Jesus said to Simon Peter, "Simon son of John, do you love me more than these?"

He answered, "Yes, Lord, you know that I love you."

Jesus said, "Feed my lambs."

Again Jesus said, "Simon son of John, do you love me?"

He answered, "Yes, Lord, you know that I love you."

Jesus said, "Take care of my sheep."

A third time he said, "Simon son of John, do you love me?"

Peter was hurt because Jesus asked him the third time, "Do you love me?"

Peter said, "Lord, you know everything; you know that I love you!" (John 21:1–17 NCV)

The Heart of His Story

Hints of God's humor are evident throughout Creation. I bet He winked at His Trinitarian self when He made the platypus; I think His face splits into a grin when He watches puppies tumble all over each other while they play; and I'm almost sure He chuckles when He watches white people dance. But I *know* Jesus is good-natured based on this post-resurrection interaction with Peter—the disciple with an embarrassing-moments list that rivals mine!

Admittedly, their conversation doesn't appear to contain much levity at first. Initially, Jesus appears less good-natured and more as though He has ADD, because He asks poor old Pete the same question three times in a row: "Simon son of John, do you love me?"

My guess is that Pete winced a little the first time. The second time he probably dropped his gaze and looked at his feet, because Christ's queries are coming just a few short days after this bumbling disciple had royally blown it. He had fallen asleep when he was supposed to be supporting Jesus while He grieved in the Garden of Gethsemane. He had lost his temper and whacked off a guy's ear with a sword.

He had chosen to save his own skin and bellowed angrily that he didn't even know Jesus, once he realized the crowd was bent on murdering the Messiah. Plus, Pete didn't just deny that he knew Jesus *once*; he exposed his yellow belly and betrayed the Savior *three* times, tossing in an expletive on the last denial just to make sure everyone listening in took the bait and swallowed the lie.

So, one would assume the third time Jesus asked Peter this question about whether he loved Him or not, questioning the former fisherman's loyalty the very same number of times he had been disloyal, that Pete would be overcome with guilt, right? The third time would be his moment of reckoning. His expression would distort with shame, and he would slink away from the scene, never to be heard from again, spending the rest of his life holed up in a dark apartment, venturing out only for cat food and a weekly therapy session.

But that's not what happened. Instead of crawling off into a cave of regret, Peter went on to help found the New Testament church, to preach the gospel of Christ everywhere he could, and ultimately to be martyred for his faith—crucified upside down, according to many historical accounts, because he didn't feel worthy to die in the same posture as his Savior before him. Pete's mistakes didn't define him, because Jesus didn't let them, which is apparent when we explore the actual Greek words Jesus and Pete spoke during what is their last recorded conversation here on earth.

While the first question is translated "Simon son of

John, do you love me?" in our English Bibles, Jesus really asked, "Simon son of John, do you *agapaō*[2] me?" In other words, "Peter, do you love me with your whole heart, with all of your emotions and your intellect?"[3]

Pete replied, "Lord, you know all things. You know I *phileō*[4] you." In other words, "Jesus, you know that I love you like a brother, with a chunk of my heart but not with all my heart and mind."[5] The second question and response mirrored the first.

But the third time, Jesus changed the verb. The third time He asked, "Simon son of John, do you *phileō* me?"

My guess is the Lamb of God had a twinkle in His eye and used a gentle tone when He probed Pete one last time. Jesus was well aware of Pete's gaffes—that when the going got tough he'd wimped out; that he failed the final exam with flying colors; that he'd fumbled the ball on the one-yard line. Instead of kicking him off the team, though, Jesus essentially said, "Hey buddy, I know you're doing the best you can and I'm not mad at you, even though you don't love Me perfectly. In fact, I'm promoting you to team captain. I'm committed to you with My whole heart, Pete. And trust Me on this, one of these days you're going to be more faithful and devoted to our cause than you can possibly imagine right now!"

Even though he was stung by the repetition of Christ's questions—and probably by the fact that Jesus had to lower the "love bar" for him—Peter didn't run off with his tail between his legs. He realized that instead of *mockery* Jesus chose to extend *mercy*. And my guess is within seconds of

Jesus asking him that third question, Pete looked back up, directly into his Savior's smiling eyes. Then he said with a grateful catch in his voice, "Oh Master, You know everything, You know I *phileō* you. But I promise I'll spend the rest of my life trying to love You better and telling anyone about You who will listen!"

Hope for Our Ongoing Stories

Just like Pete, I've received winks from Jesus when I really deserved a whack. I make lots of mistakes, such as sprawling and yelping in public unwittingly. But I also make plenty of blunders *willfully*. I often stumble on rebellious trails I've stubbornly chosen for myself as opposed to the path toward which the Holy Spirit shepherded me. Even still, our Savior is kind. Most of the time He doesn't raise His voice or send me to time-out. Instead, He helps me back to my feet with a patient grin, dusts me off, and then applies divine Neosporin to my skinned heart. And only later, after I'm no longer wobbly and the scabs have healed, will my Prince gently tease me about being the bride who tripped all the way down the aisle. His gracious good humor is part of what makes my blooper reel of a story so bearable, and even so enjoyable.

Living in Light of His Story

Dear Jesus, thank You for choosing to look past my faults and false starts. Thank You for being slow to anger and rich in good humor. Please help me to be more like Peter—to use Your undeserved compassion as a catalyst to live out my faith with more vim and vigor. May the grace You have for my gaffes motivate me to lean more fully into You. Amen.

Personal Reflection and/or Group Discussion Questions

1. What typically gets you tickled?

2. Describe the last time you laughed so hard you cried?

3. What are some of the *hints of God's humor* you've noticed in the world around you?

4. Read Proverbs 17:22. Why do you think humor is good for our hearts?

5. Read Luke 6:21. Why do you think Jesus connected the dots between weeping now and laughing later?

6. How can good humor help us keep an eternal perspective during earthly trials?

7. Do you think people who are able to chuckle at their own frailties are more compassionate when their friends and families make mistakes? Why?

8. Read Proverbs 31:15. Do you think those closest to you would say that verse describes you too? If so, why are you able to grin at the calendar?

Journal Entry

Please consider completing this sentence in your personal journal:

So, today I've been thinking about Your good humor, how Your eyes probably crinkle at the corners when You're watching me, Jesus, and . . .

chapter 9
WHO'S GOT YOUR BACK?

Jesus does not want us floating through space or sitting in front of our televisions. Jesus wants us interacting, eating together, laughing together, praying together. Loneliness is something that came with the fall.[1]

—Donald Miller

So, today I've been thinking about the gift of community. Specifically, I've been reflecting on how grateful I am to be part of a close-knit crew of four other women. Even though we're not related, the five of us started referring to ourselves as "the cousins" a year or so after we started hanging out together in Nashville. It may sound silly, but *cousin* seems to adequately describe the familial bond we share, especially on Sunday nights when we gather in one or the other of our homes and eat dinner together. There's just something about having a handful of people you love, and who love you back, breaking bread and breathing the same air for a while.

Last week everybody congregated at my cottage in the country. We lingered over spicy chili and cornbread and ended up savoring slices of chocolate pie around a bonfire together. Some might question my choice to have people over to share a meal just a few hours after arriving home from a cross-country flight after being at a Women of Faith conference all weekend, but consistent community is what helps keep me sane. Knowing Kelly was sitting by the fireplace in my living room poring over Old Testament commentaries, April and Mary Katharine were watching the Titans football game in the den, and Paige was in the backyard lighting the fire pit, helped settle my jet-lagged heart into the happy hum of belonging while I set the table.

Catholic priest and author John F. O'Grady elevated sharing a meal to a sort of sacrament when he wrote, "Salvation is not reserved for the future alone. It is present when a family sits down at a family celebration in thanksgiving for the goodness they have received and the goodness they contribute to each other and enjoy fine food and good wine and great company."[2] Unlike Rev. O'Grady, I didn't used to think carving out time to engage in a weekly meal and deep conversation with the same small group of people was that important. And since I was raised Baptist, I sure didn't think wine played a role in community! Although I've been blessed with lots of dear friends through the years,

I never realized how much I needed to have an ongoing connection with a family of fellow sojourners.

That is, I didn't realize it until I suffered a loss that knocked me off my feet, until I was so emotionally wrecked that pouring my heart out to a counselor or one person at a time wasn't cutting it. Individual friends didn't have enough hands to help me gather up all the broken pieces. If I had tried to lean on just one person during that painful season, I probably would have flattened her. I needed a cohesive posse of prayer and compassion. I needed the Christian version of AA or *Cheers*—a place where everybody knew my name and my junk. Frankly, I think we all do.

One of my favorite onscreen moments that illustrates the necessity of community takes place at the end of the Academy Award—winning movie *Little Miss Sunshine*, actress Abigail Breslin plays the role of seven-year-old Olive, the youngest child in a comically dysfunctional family. Her dad, Richard Hoover (played by Greg Kinnear), is a wannabe motivational speaker who is inept at supporting his family financially but very gifted when it comes to spouting pithy catchphrases. Her hardworking mom, Sheryl (played by Toni Collette), is frazzled and exasperated with her dad. Her older brother, Dwayne (played by Paul Dano), has stubbornly retreated into a world of silence and only communicates by writing messages on a notepad. Her brilliant but paranoid uncle, Frank (played by Steve Carell), has moved in with them following his nervous breakdown. And her beloved grandfather, Edwin (played by Alan Arkin), is a supportive but raunchy old fellow who lives with them because he was kicked out of his retirement community for dealing drugs.

This quirky film (which I *can't* heartily recommend because of the language and some explicit content) chronicles the Hoovers' madcap adventures on a road trip from their home in Albuquerque, New Mexico, to Redondo Beach, California, where Olive has earned the right to compete in the Little Miss Sunshine pageant, which she has her heart set on winning. Hilarity (they're traveling in a dilapidated VW microbus) and tragedy (the grandfather dies en route) ensue, and against all odds they make it to California in the nick of time for the pageant. But when pudgy, pale, Coke-bottle-eyeglass-wearing Olive happily clomps onstage alongside the other young, polished, beauty queen contenders, it's painfully obvious to everyone but *her* that she's out of her league.

And things go from bad to worse during the talent portion of the competition, because Olive enthusiastically begins a bawdy routine Edwin had secretly taught her to the accompaniment of the infamous Rick James song "Super Freak." Of course, the other moms and dads in the audience gasp as Olive innocently gyrates to the suggestive lyrics. Teenagers began to titter. The judges can't tear their shocked gazes away from the grinning, hip-thrusting little girl. Everyone in the second-rate hotel ballroom is uncomfortable, including Olive's family. You can tell by the embarrassed expressions on Richard's, Sheryl's, Frank's, and Dwayne's faces that, at first, they are tempted to flee. Instead, one by one they stand up and begin to clap to the beat of the trashy tune. Then all four of them rush forward and join her onstage. They begin dancing too, encircling her with their wagons of unconditional love and support. All the while, Olive joyfully wiggles on, completely oblivious to the scandal she has created, her face radiant with belonging.

Such is the gift of true community—a wee tribe of people who will cheer for us, not necessarily because we're good, but because they claim us as theirs. *Jesus gives us the gift of true community*.

JESUS AND THE GIFT OF COMMUNITY

A few days later, when Jesus again entered Capernaum, the people heard that he had come home. So many gathered that there was no room left, not even outside the door, and he preached the word to them. Some men came, bringing to him a paralytic, carried by four of them. Since they could not get him to Jesus because of the crowd, they made an opening in the roof above Jesus and, after digging through it, lowered the mat the paralyzed man was lying on. When Jesus saw their faith, he said to the paralytic, "Son, your sins are forgiven." (Mark 2:1–5)

The Heart of His Story
Before we dive into this short-yet-sweet miracle at the beginning of Mark's gospel account, let's review the proper theological framework for the physical healings recorded in the Bible. I think lots of well-intentioned Christians have

either an underrealized or an overrealized *eschatology*—"any system of doctrines concerning last or final matters, such as death, the Judgment, the future state, etc."[3]—regarding healing miracles. An *underrealized* eschatology is the belief system that compartmentalizes or subjugates Christ's healing miracles as "tricks" He performed to persuade people to believe in Him. An *overrealized* eschatology would be to assume that, if diseased or disabled persons just had enough faith, they could be healed instantaneously.

Neither view is biblically accurate. Jesus wasn't a magician, pulling healings out of His proverbial hat to impress partygoers, nor was He a manipulative snake-oil salesman with a tent and a collapsible pulpit, who held healings up like carrots before rabbits so as to coerce gullible believers into praying harder or writing bigger checks. He didn't perform on command (John 6:25–33), and He was always motivated by compassion.

The best way I know how to frame the healing miracles of Jesus is by quoting the speech I've heard hundreds of times from the lips of a typically bored flight attendant: "Please turn off all electronic devices at this time—all laptops, iPods, iPads, BlackBerries, and blueberries. Anything with an on/off switch. Please raise your seat backs and tray tables to their original upright positions. Crew members will be making one last trip through the cabin to pick up any remaining cups, trash, or newspapers. We will be landing in Nashville shortly." That familiar monologue never fails to make my heart sigh with relief, because it means I'm almost home. In much the same way, our Savior's healing miracles point to our true home—they hint at mankind's future, glorified condition in heaven when we will be immune to sickness and decay. They serve to stimulate faith and to reward faith. And in the case of Mark 2, the miracle Jesus bestowed rewarded the faith of a whole posse of friends.

The setting for this healing is literally "in the house" in Capernaum, which was a town on the northern shore of the Sea of Galilee that had become the Messiah's home base. That meant Jesus was probably staying in the house of one of His disciples or, perhaps, the house some generous follower let Him use when He was in town. Furthermore, by this time in His earthly ministry, Jesus had earned quite a reputation as a rabbi and a healer. News of His attendance-record—breaking revivals was posted on Facebook and Twitter. An e-mail describing the way He touched a leper, whose skin then became as pink and smooth as a baby's cheek, had been forwarded throughout Israel. So, when word spread that Jesus was coming back to Capernaum, a big crowd gathered where He was staying. They trampled the rose bushes and elbowed each other in their quest to get as close to Him as possible.

Of course, not everyone assembled was a true follower of Christ. Some were just curious, like the rubbernecks who slow down to a crawl on the interstate and gawk at minor accidents, wondering what this traveling evangelist was up to. And some were surely there to spy on the Messiah. No doubt there were Pharisees and other rabbis in the crowd, eyeing Jesus with envy and suspicion. They were probably hoping to catch Him in some transgression of the Law or a slip of the tongue. But some were passionate believers in Jesus and His ability to restore broken hearts and broken bodies. In fact, four followers were so ardent in their belief that, when they couldn't make a path through the throng to get their paralyzed pal close to Christ, they scrambled onto the roof and began hacking a hole in it.

Wouldn't you have loved to see the faces in that packed house when chunks of mud and straw started raining down on their heads? I wonder what expression Jesus Himself was wearing when He paused in the middle of His sermon, knowing full well what was going on overhead. I'm guessing His face split into a grin when the hole widened enough for one of those four men to poke his head through and announce, "Lord, we're really sorry to drop in like this, but our buddy is pretty messed up, and we'd be much obliged if You could see fit to fix him." When they lowered their pallet filled with precious cargo, Mark reported that Jesus was moved—so moved He immediately healed the wounded member of their tribe. The four's faith in Christ, combined with their loyalty to a friend, formed the amalgamation of a jaw-dropping miracle.

Hope for Our Ongoing Stories

One of my dearest friends for the past twenty-five years is also a paralytic. Her name is Eva Whittington Self, and although her legs don't work, she's much faster than I at moving toward God, which is one of the millions of reasons I'm crazy about her. But our relationship isn't all about prayer and fasting. We also like shopping and eating. And often, to the chagrin of her even-tempered husband, Andrew, normalcy morphs into adventure when we're together.

For instance, a few years ago we were staying in a hotel in downtown Chattanooga when the fire alarm went off at two o'clock in the morning, followed by the ominous announcement that there was an actual fire in the building and everyone needed to evacuate immediately. Eva and I scrambled out of our room into the hallway and then came to an abrupt halt at the elevator, realizing it was sealed off, and we were going to have to somehow get her down fourteen flights of stairs, because we were on the seventh floor.

Eva blurted something selfless like, "Go ahead, Lisa; a security guard will be here any minute to help me."

I replied something along the lines of, "Fat chance, sugar," because there was no way I was going to abandon the only person who will gobble copious amounts of carbohydrates with me when I'm sad.

After a quick Lucy-and-Ethel kind of embrace, we rolled/ran to the stairwell, and I grabbed the closest big guy I could find and told him we needed help. He nodded solemnly as I rattled off instructions regarding where and how to grab Eva's wheelchair without tipping her over backward, and within seconds the three of us were descending as a bulky unit. It was a long haul down, and I had to correct our new friend on his toting methods several times, and he responded with mumbled expletives, but we eventually made it out to the parking lot at the same time firemen were racing into the hotel. The three of us talked for a few minutes in the red glow of the fire truck's strobe light, and then after awkwardly receiving our profuse gratitude, Mr. Cussy-pants ambled off toward his buddies.

As she watched him walk away, Eva said, "I forgot to ask him where he's from. He had such an interesting accent, and I couldn't quite place it."

Breathing easily for the first time in a while, I said, "He didn't have an accent, Eva; he was drunk as a skunk!"

I prefer a noninebriated posse, but when you desperately need to be lifted, you can't be too picky! And quite frankly, I consider anyone who'll walk, roll, crawl, or carry heavy stuff with me through tough times to be a treasure, especially if they're helping me move toward our Redeemer. As bishop and theologian Lesslie Newbigin once wisely wrote, "The congregation is the hermeneutic of the Gospel."[4] In other words, we formulate our understanding of who Jesus is largely through the lens of community. The people God positions around us can be amazing carriers of His grace.

Living in Light of His Story

Dear Jesus, thank You for the gift of friendship. For the dear men and women who've helped lug me through life when I was too weak or scared or overwhelmed to propel myself alone. Please help me to be a better friend to my "pallet pals" by being slower to take offense and faster to forgive. And please help me to be more sensitive to those who need a lift, the ones who are having a hard time getting close to You on their own. Amen.

Personal Reflection and/or Group Discussion Questions

1. Who would you describe as integral members of your tribe in this season of your life?

2. If you had to choose a tribe mascot, what would it be? What does your mascot symbolize about your community?

3. Ecclesiastes 4:9–12. What's the most authentic and supportive multicorded community (three or more close-knit friends) of which you've gotten to be a part? What do you think was/is the key to your cohesiveness?

4. During His earthly ministry, Jesus engaged in relationships in a concentric model of intimacy (like a

target). For example, God the Father and the Holy Spirit were His bull's-eye, the very center of His circle. The three people closest to Him—Peter, James, and John—formed the second innermost ring. The third "band of connection" included the other disciples. The fourth ring included dear friends like Lazarus, whom Jesus loved but didn't spend as much time with, and so on. Do your relationships fall into a similar target-type pattern?

5. Have you ever experienced one of those especially tough seasons when, if you had tried to lean on just one person, you probably would have flattened her? If so, who were the friends who "hacked through the roof" for you?

6. Read John 13:34–35. Author Henri Nouwen wrote, "Everyone who returns from a long and difficult trip is looking for someone waiting for him at the station or the airport."[5] Who do you think would name you as their faithful "airport friend" this year?

Journal Entry

Please consider completing this sentence in your personal journal:

So, today I've been thinking about Your generous gift of true friendships, Jesus, and . . .

chapter 10
BUSYNESS ISN'T A SPIRITUAL GIFT

Today the heart of God is an open wound of love. He aches over our distance and preoccupation. He mourns that we do not draw near to him. He grieves that we have forgotten him. He weeps over our obsession with muchness and manyness. He longs for our presence.[1]

—Richard Foster

So, today I've been thinking about the gift of rest.

But even as I typed those words I found myself smiling sheepishly, fully aware that it would be appropriate for God to zap me with a lightning bolt right now because the past few months have been among the busiest I've ever experienced.

As a matter of fact, some days have been so jam-packed that my brain has started to boycott the pace and is refusing to participate.

For instance, last week while I was running errands, I parked my car and then spent at least thirty seconds staring at a lime-green sticky note on the passenger seat beside me that had the words "Male Stuff" written on it with an asterisk. I recognized my own handwriting but couldn't for the life of me remember what I meant when I wrote it. *Male stuff . . . hm.* I'm forty-seven and single. I've never been married and like to tease that my husband is lost and won't stop for directions. So, buying man supplies isn't part of my normal routine.

I stared at that little neon note and wondered if maybe I needed a leaf blower or a hammer or a new remote control for the television. I wondered if maybe my dad called the night before, after I'd taken Ambien, and told me he was coming to visit, which meant I probably needed to go to the grocery store and buy some boy food like Cheetos or polish sausage or beef jerky. *Male stuff . . . hm.* It wasn't until I looked up and noticed I was parked right outside the post office that I realized I'd been so harried when I wrote my to-do list I'd misspelled the word *mail*!

Unfortunately, memory spasms like that have been happening on a regular basis this season. I lost my keys yesterday and I've literally never lost my keys before. Of course, that's probably because with two remotes (one for the car and one for the alarm system), nine keys, and an assortment of little plastic doohickeys that save me all of twenty cents every time I shop at the grocery stores represented by the doohickeys, my key ring weighs more than Paris Hilton's dog and is almost as big as my head. One would assume that finding such a large wad of metal in a relatively clean house would be easy. Alas, I've looked everywhere—in drawers, under every cushion, and even in the freezer—for those keys and can't find them anywhere. I think I'm going to have to break down and buy one of those metal detectors that old guys who wear shorts and orthopedic shoes with black socks to the beach are so fond of having.

The bottom line is, I'm often too busy. I tend to write more checks than my mental and physical banks can cash. Mind you, most of the commitments on my calendar are good things. Aside from those pesky boy food shopping sprees, I spend most of my time preparing to speak at Christian women's conferences ("est-fests," or estrogen festivals, for the uninitiated), traveling approximately 160 days a year to and from said conferences, writing books and magazine articles about faith-related issues, reading great literature so as to become a better writer (so that someone besides my mother will actually read what I write), and volunteering at a halfway house for women transitioning from prison to independent living. I mean, I'm not out there burning the midnight oil as a blackjack dealer or anything; I'm hustling around for *kingdom purposes*.

So what gives? Why doesn't God give me a more dedicated brain and a less sleep-dependent body to handle my "calling"? You're probably way ahead of me and already know the answer to that question. Our heavenly Father is not some insensitive CEO pushing His minions for more bankable hours. He cares far more about the posture of our hearts than our productivity. Even "good" things can become the enemy of God's best for us.

Furthermore, our Creator encourages us to make time for rest time because He knows we tend to get burned out when we have too many irons in the fire. Losing your train of thought and your keys is no big deal compared to what a dear friend recently lost. She got so distracted by her manic schedule that she began to misplace her values and started having an affair and is now losing her marriage. The seemingly innocuous habit of busyness, of going too fast and too long without a break, is what muffled the spiritual alarms she'd heeded in the past and sent her skidding out of control into an intersection of immorality that has completely wrecked her life and her family.

My friend's sexual derailment and its heartbreaking consequences trumpeted a shrill warning for me to slow down. Take more deep breaths. Pray. Listen to God's guiding voice. And pay closer attention to the anxious thoughts running through my mind and the selfish feelings lodged in my soul, which are contrary to what God says. I am determined to finish the race He's set for me, even if it means not running as fast as I can. I want to live a full life at a calmer, less frenzied pace.

So I'm sitting here this morning with my laptop open. I've returned lots of e-mails and booked two flights for future events. I've read three academic articles that pertain to what I'm currently writing and have cleaned my room. But I've also gotten up to put more logs on the fire; I've spent several minutes staring out the kitchen window at the freezing sheets of winter rain; I've drunk deeply from Sarah Young's wonderful devotional *Jesus Calling*, while sipping my favorite French-pressed coffee; and although it's almost noon, I'm still wearing pajamas!

Our Redeemer's gift of rest allows us to fulfill our responsibilities while maintaining inner peace and intimacy with God.

JESUS AND THE GIFT OF REST

Jesus now called the Twelve and gave them authority and power to deal with all the demons and cure diseases. He commissioned them to preach the news of God's kingdom and heal the sick. He said, "Don't load yourselves up with equipment. Keep it simple; you are the equipment. And no luxury inns—get a modest place and be content there until you leave. If you're not welcomed, leave town. Don't make a scene. Shrug your shoulders and move on."

Commissioned, they left. They traveled from town to town telling the latest news of God, the Message, and curing people everywhere they went.

Herod, the ruler, heard of these goings on and didn't know what to think. There were people saying John had come back from the dead, others that Elijah had appeared, still others that some prophet of long ago had shown up. Herod said, "But I killed John—took off his head. So who is this that I keep hearing about?" Curious, he looked for a chance to see him in action.

> The apostles returned and reported on what they had done. Jesus took them away, off by themselves, near the town called Bethsaida. (Luke 9:1–10 MSG)

The Heart of His Story

Dr. Luke doesn't specify just how frazzled or brain-drained the disciples were at this point, but they certainly had legitimate reasons to be exhausted. They had been on a long mission trip with a twofold purpose: to *heal* the sick and to *herald*—or preach—the gospel. And in submission to how Jesus had commissioned them, they had traipsed all over the Galilean region caring for the physically sick, the mentally ill, and the spiritually hopeless without any provisions for their own comfort. When we read more traditional translations of Luke 9, we find out the disciples didn't carry staffs, traveler's bags, bread, money, or even a second tunic on their journey to share the message of the Christ. That meant they took nothing more than what was absolutely necessary. No coolers filled with snacks and Gatorade. No iPods. Not even a change of clothes.

I went on a mission trip last summer where we didn't have air-conditioning in our hotel or toilet paper in the restrooms of the schools and orphanages we visited. Of course, we'd come to Honduras with roller bags full of clean clothes, fans, granola bars, and wet wipes, but we still thought we were roughing it! I can't imagine listening to the sad stories of suffering people, serving watery soup to hungry children, and laying hands on lepers all day long while not being sure of where I'd lay my own head that night or where my next meal was coming from as the disciples did.

Plus, Jesus told His disciples they had to be content wherever they stayed, which gives me the shivers because I've been housed in some pretty sketchy places through the years. Once an event planner decided to surprise me by booking a room at a bed-and-breakfast that had just opened for business in her small town. When we arrived, the inn hostess was nowhere to be found, so her husband reluctantly turned off his chainsaw and set it on the ground beside the pile of wood he was cutting in the backyard to usher us to their "rented room." Clad in a filthy undershirt and sawdust-covered jeans, he gestured to a wall of odiferous trash bags next to the side door and said gruffly, "Sorry 'bout that."

Then he led us through the kitchen, where another disheveled man was frying baloney and two toddlers with very dirty diapers were chasing each other around a table screeching. Finally, he clomped up a narrow staircase to what was surely the room Cinderella's attic dwelling had been modeled after and shooed a mangy cat off the frayed bedspread and said, "Here's where you'll be staying." I can promise you that what I felt wasn't anything close to contentment and I quickly made up an excuse about being allergic to cats and paid for my own room at a nearby Fairfield Inn!

But Peter and company didn't have the option of checking into a budget hotel. They stayed with whoever would have them, probably sleeping on dirt floors more often than not. And I'm sure they would have been thrilled to receive a slice of fried luncheon meat. Compounding their bare bones road-trip stress, verse 5 implies they didn't receive warm welcomes everywhere they went either. Some of the villages they visited were full of people with crossed arms and closed doors. Sometimes there were hecklers in the crowds to whom they preached. Perhaps even a few stone-throwers.

After weeks of grueling, itinerant ministry work, the apostles received word that John the Baptist had been murdered, and the last wisps of wind evaporated from their sails. They had labored hard and accomplished their purpose but now the needles on their physical and emotional gas tanks were hovering close to empty. So they turned around and headed home to have their batteries recharged by the comfort and encouragement of being alone with Jesus. I imagine them pulling into the driveway to find Him standing there waiting. All twelve men spill out of the cramped church van and gather around the Savior, clamoring for His attention, trying to talk over each other about the miracles they had witnessed and the people with whom they had prayed.

I can picture Jesus smiling affectionately throughout their boisterous commentary. I can picture His helping unload their few dusty belongings and getting them settled back into their dorm rooms. When the chatter slowed down and their eyelids started to droop, I can almost hear Jesus saying tenderly: "Come off by yourselves; let's take a break and get a little rest" (Mark 6:31 MSG). My guess is that our gentle Shepherd then tiptoed from room to room pulling blankets over each of His dozen friends as they began to snore.

Hope for Our Ongoing Stories

I'm so glad Jesus advocated rest for His followers. He doesn't guilt us into overdoing it even when it comes to ministry. Instead, He teaches us (and modeled for us according to Mark 1:35 and Luke 4:42) to slow down and recuperate after giving our all for the sake of the gospel. To find a balance between *going out and doing* and *being still and knowing*. Resting—learning to weave practical Sabbaths into our schedules—isn't a punitive decree; it's God's generous endowment for our protection and perseverance. And I think Matthew narrated Jesus' words regarding this gift better than anyone else:

> Are you tired? Worn out? Burned out on religion? Come to me. Get away with me and you'll recover your life. I'll show you how to take a real rest. Walk with me and work with me—watch how I do it. Learn the unforced rhythms of grace. I won't lay anything heavy or ill-fitting on you. Keep company with me and you'll learn to live freely and lightly. (Matthew 11:28–30 MSG)

Living in Light of His Story

Slow me down, Lord.

Ease the pounding of my heart by the quieting of my mind.

Steady my hurried pace with a vision of the eternal reach of time.

Give me, amid the confusion of the day, the calmness of the everlasting hills.

Break the tension of my nerves and muscles with the soothing music of the singing streams that live in my memory.

Teach me the art of taking minute vacations—of slowing down to look at a flower, to chat with a friend, to pat a dog, to smile at a child, to read a few lines from a good book.

Slow me down, Lord, and inspire me to send my roots deep into the soil of life's enduring values, that I may grow toward my greater destiny.

Remind me each day that the race is not always to the swift; that there is more to life than increasing its speed.

Let me look upward to the towering oak and know that it grew great and strong because it grew slowly and well.[2]

—WILFRED A. PETERSON

Personal Reflection and/or Group Discussion Questions

1. On the scale of one to ten below regarding busyness—with one being "couch potato" and ten being "racing

around like a chicken with your head cut off"—circle the number that represents where you would place yourself.

1   2   3   4   5   6   7   8   9   10

2. Read Psalm 23. Now reread verse 2. What do you think David meant when he wrote that the Shepherd "makes us lie down"?

3. How would you grade yourself on the subject of real rest? Does learning to be quiet in God's presence come naturally for you, or do you have to work at it?

4. Do you think real spiritual rest always involves a complete cessation of activity? Explain your answer.

5. Read Hebrews 4:11–13 and 1 Corinthians 10:1–13. How would you describe the relationship between obedience and rest?

6. Describe your own personal "green pasture" and "still waters"—the places and spaces where you go when you need to unwind and be alone with God.

7. What are the most practical ways you've learned to practice the art of rest, of being still and knowing that He is God in the midst of your busy life?

Journal Entry

Please consider completing this sentence in your personal journal:

So, today I've been thinking about the much-needed gift of real rest You offer us, Jesus, and . . .

part 3
REAL GROWTH

chapter 11
EMPATHIZING WITH ENEMIES

*The heartfelt compassion that hastens forgiveness matures when we
discover where our enemy cries.*[1]

—Brennan Manning

So, today I've been thinking about becoming less
critical.

Which is a lofty goal considering that we're plopped
on a planet with so many irritating people, which brings
to mind a story my friend Yvonne told me. Her father was
incarcerated and wasn't fond of most of the other felons
with whom he served time. And the close quarters of the
Indiana prison system only served to exacerbate his aversion
to men he deemed "morons" and "idiots." One day, when
Yvonne was encouraging him to be more patient with his

fellow inmates, especially given the fact that he was going to be rubbing shoulders with them for a very long time, he fumed, "They're taking up too much air!"

I find it incredulous that a man convicted of attempted murder could begrudge someone else's habit of inhaling and exhaling. Yet my sensitivity to morons and idiots is no less self-righteous or unwarranted. For instance, here are the three biggest irritants I've dealt with this week:

A loud-talking woman, sitting nearby at Starbucks, raved on and on in a grating, nasally voice about how her husband left the mail in a messy pile on their kitchen table. Since I rarely have thirty minutes to savor a nonfat-with-whip mocha and leisurely read through *USA Today*, I looked for another place to sit far away from Barbara the Bellower, but there were no other seats available. So I tried to focus on the stories I was reading in the newspaper and tune her out, which was not unlike dragging a lawn chair up to the edge of a runway and then trying to ignore the roar of planes taking off and landing. Eventually, I succumbed to heavy sighs and sideways glances, hoping she'd get the hint and lower her voice, or at least change the subject to something remotely interesting.

Then there was the giant, garrulous man who stepped *on* me while attempting to step *over* me and wedge himself into the middle seat of the exit row for our four-and-a-half-hour flight from Portland to Nashville. He was initially sitting in the aisle seat behind me, next to his saintly wife, but after a few fidgety minutes he crowed, "Hey, honey, you don't mind if I take that seat up there, do you? Because it has more leg room."

Of course, once he settled his bulk into the narrow

middle berth, he stuck his right, tree trunk–sized leg into the hole underneath the seat in front of me, commandeered the armrest between us, and eventually drooped his massive head onto my shoulder when he fell asleep. I suppose I should have been grateful he didn't drool, or I would have surely drowned. Instead, I was annoyed by his imposition and spent the better part of the flight leaning uncomfortably into the aisle or walking slowly to and from the rear lavatory.

Finally, *there was the scowling woman* behind the wheel of a white Honda who refused to let any other drivers merge into her lane, even though we were in a construction zone on the interstate and there was a blinking yellow sign informing motorists to MERGE into a single lane. As the rest of us backed up into an indignant clump in the median, too close to the orange barrels for comfort, I wished for the hundredth time that cars came equipped with inflatable bumpers, so we could plow into piggish, grumpy drivers and knock them out of the way. Or maybe in the same way people convicted of drunk driving have to wear those orange vests while they clean up trash on the roadside, bad drivers could roll around in vehicles swathed in orange vinyl with "Horrible Driver" emblazoned on all sides!

When I consider that the three people who irked me recently were a woman who talked too loudly and too long; a chunky, claustrophobic flyer; and a lady with bad driving habits, I have to admit I'm getting on my own nerves because all of those aggravating little quirks abound in me! The old proverb "When you point out somebody else's flaws, you've got three fingers pointing back at you" comes to mind. That encourages me to be more lethargic when it comes to taking offense and to remember I'm only reading the tiniest paragraph in their stories. Maybe the verbose woman with too much volume in Starbucks has a hearing problem and rarely gets to converse with other people in social settings. Maybe middle-seat-man really does have issues with small spaces because his mean mama punished him by locking him into a closet when he was a child. Maybe the lady who wouldn't share her lane on I-65 was coming home from the doctor's office and preoccupied with how she was going to tell her husband and children that the lump in her breast was malignant. Maybe if I knew their *whole* stories, including the sore spots and sad chapters, I wouldn't be so quick to judge them as inferior.

A few days ago, right smack in the middle of my juggernaut of judgment, I began thumbing through *Bird by Bird*, one of my favorite books by Anne Lamott. Within moments it fell open to a dog-eared page with the following truism highlighted in yellow: "You can safely assume you've created God in your own image when it turns out that God hates all the same people you do."[2] I sat there stunned with fresh conviction for a few moments and then a deep sigh of relief welled up in my soul. I'm so glad God doesn't hate who I hate. More specifically, I'm so glad Jesus isn't irritated by the people who irritate me. If He were, surely He would also roll His eyes in exasperation a million times a day over *my* gaffes. Yet, instead of making angels guffaw in glory by mocking our foolishness, mercy reigns in our Redeemer. Jesus never forgets our sore spots or sad chapters.

We can become less critical by choosing to focus on the whole of other people's stories as opposed to one irritating chapter.

How Jesus Helps Us Become Less Critical

Jesus went to the Mount of Olives. But early in the morning he went back to the Temple, and all the people came to him, and he sat and taught them. The teachers of the law and the Pharisees brought a woman who had been caught in adultery. They forced her to stand before the people. They said to Jesus, "Teacher, this woman was caught having sexual relations with a man who is not her husband. The law of Moses commands that we stone to death every woman who does this. What do you say we should do?" They were asking this to trick Jesus so that they could have some charge against him.

But Jesus bent over and started writing on the ground with his finger. When they continued to ask Jesus their question, he raised up and said, "Anyone here who has never sinned can throw the first stone at her." Then Jesus bent over again and wrote on the ground.

Those who heard Jesus began to leave one by one, first the older men and then the others. Jesus was left there alone with the woman standing before him. Jesus raised up again and asked her, "Woman, where are they? Has no one judged you guilty?"

She answered, "No one, sir."

Then Jesus said, "I also don't judge you guilty. You may go now, but don't sin anymore." (John 8:1–11 NCV)

The Heart of His Story

I have a crystal-clear picture of this woman and her world in my imagination. I envision her to have been in her mid-forties with shoulder-length brown hair. She was single and dedicated to her job, having worked her way up the ladder from secretary to assistant regional manager at Widgets R Us. Her stingy, hairpiece-wearing boss had denied her pay-raise requests for the past several years but finally allowed her to move into a larger cubicle where she artfully arranged pictures of her three-legged dog Lucky, a cheery fern, and several motivational plaques. And sitting discreetly on her bookshelf was a *Living Bible* from which she read during the weekly voluntary devotions she lead with the small team of telemarketers she managed. Her name was Liz.

One day a girlfriend called and asked if Liz wanted to go to a new singles' worship night at a megachurch across town. Liz declined, explaining that she had sworn off all singles' activities and had never met anyone she was interested in dating at church anyway.

Her friend persisted and said, "Liz, this is really different, I promise! The music is awesome, the teaching is incredible, and there will be like five hundred people there, including a ton of Christian guys in their forties!"

Liz sighed and agreed to go but decided rather pessimistically that she wouldn't put much effort into getting dressed up for the occasion. Instead, she would wear minimal makeup and her most comfortable elastic-waist pants.

Liz instantly regretted her decision when she and her three unmarried, middle-aged girlfriends walked into the sanctuary of the First Bapticostal Community Church with Cup Holders, because there *were* lots of normal-looking men her age milling around! Her heart swelled with anticipation as she noticed none of them were wearing pocket protectors, and only three or four had brought their mothers. The night kept exceeding her expectations, because the music really was wonderful, and the Bible teacher really was engaging. Then, to top it all off, a guy whom one of the friends she came with knew from a spinning class at the Y asked if she and her girlfriends wanted to go to Denny's for coffee and pie afterward with his buddies and him. The girls readily agreed, and Liz could hardly believe her luck when she ended up seated across from a friendly guy with big dimples named Larry.

Their party of eight stayed at Denny's laughing and talking much longer than they'd planned and Liz fell into bed around midnight exhausted but happy. She daydreamed about Larry at work the next day, thinking, *I'm not sure if he has much money, and he definitely doesn't have much hair, but he sure is funny*. Of course, she went back to the singles' worship night the following week, this time with new highlights in her hair and wearing control-top designer jeans. She pretended not to notice Larry when she walked in to find a seat but had a hard time maintaining her poker face when he stood up and called her name, motioning for her to sit by him. And just like that, Liz and Larry became an item. They sat together every Tuesday night and, instead of going to Denny's with the rest of their crowd, began going to Olive Garden afterward to giggle and stare into each other's eyes.

But three months after they started dating, Liz and Larry stopped going to the singles' worship night and started meeting at a Holiday Inn Express on the edge of town instead. Liz felt conflicted about sleeping with Larry, especially since she found out he was married. She quieted the questions in her heart by repeating his mantra about how awful his wife was and how surely God wanted them to be together.

Early one Wednesday morning, Liz was staring up at the stained ceiling tiles in their hotel room while Larry snored away, wondering if he really would leave his wife and marry her after Larry Jr. graduated from high school, when she heard a keycard in the door. She thought distractedly, *Why is the maid coming to clean now?* until the door flew open, and it wasn't the maid at all. It was five men with angry expressions in cheap suits. Before she could react, they stormed into the love nest and jerked her out of bed. When she whirled around frantically to grab a sheet or a pillow to cover her naked body, she saw Larry accepting a wad of bills from one of the used-car-salesmen look-alikes. So the whole time they were dragging her down the hallway, across the parking lot, and toward the temple courts, all she could think was, *I thought he loved me. I thought he loved me. I thought he loved me.*

I've obviously taken a lot of liberty with that New

Testament story but the scene might have been similar. In light of her "boyfriend's" absence in the Bible story, many scholars teach that it's likely that a man set up the woman in John 8 since, according to the law the Pharisees were citing, *both* the man and the woman found guilty of adultery were liable for stoning (Leviticus 20:10). She wasn't just some sinner who'd been caught red-handed. She was a heartbroken sinner who'd been caught red-handed. Which makes Jesus' action of bending over and scribbling in the sand all the more meaningful, because when He did so, everyone's eyes shifted from boring into her with judgment and scorn to looking at what He was writing. It provided her first chance to adjust the sheet to make sure her private parts were covered up. To catch her breath. To find her last shred of dignity. Squatting down to doodle in the dirt is one of the most merciful things Jesus could have done for *that* woman in *that* moment.

My guess is her prodigal heart had softened to repentance before the crowd ever dispersed and Jesus pronounced her free to go.

Hope for Our Ongoing Stories

For the sake of the gospel and the sake of the mistake-prone people we rub shoulders with every day, Christians have to recognize that Christ alone has the perfect combination of righteousness and compassion to stand in judgment of the human heart. We have to remember the only One worthy of condemning us chose instead to pardon us. Only then—when we're honest about the fact that apart from God's grace we deserve to be damned too—will we find ourselves extending kindness instead of criticism. Only then will we be able to empty our bulging pockets of rocks.

Living in Light of His Story

Dear Jesus, the woman caught in adultery reminds me so much of myself. My sin is every bit as black as hers; I've just never been publicly exposed like that. Thank You for disciplining me privately and forgiving me lavishly. Thank You for applying holy ointment to my wounds instead of rubbing salt in them. Only the velvet chains of Your love can keep my wandering heart faithful. So I pray as David, please hem me in behind and before, Lord. And help me to extend some small measure of the grace You've given me to the people You place in my path. Amen.

Personal Reflection and/or Group Discussion Questions

1. What's at the very top of your this-bugs-me list?

2. How would you paraphrase Anne Lamott's assertion: "You can safely assume you've created God in your own image when it turns out that God hates all the same people you do"?

3. Describe a situation in which you were tempted to sling a stone at someone's reputation. What happened?

4. Read 2 Samuel 16:5–14 and 2 Samuel 19:14–23. How would you summarize the moral of this true story about being unfairly pelted with rocks?

5. What verbal rocks are you most prone to throw? What verbal rocks thrown at you have left the darkest bruises on your heart?

6. Do you agree or disagree with the statement that "Christians are the only ones who shoot their wounded"? Explain your answer.

7. Read Ephesians 4:29 and Romans 12:15–16. Describe how someone used words to help you heal—instead of adding insult to injury—during a difficult season?

Journal Entry

Please consider completing this sentence in your personal journal:

So, today I've been thinking about becoming less critical and judgmental, Jesus, and . . .

chapter 12
LIAR, LIAR! PANTS ON FIRE!

How we view ourselves at any given moment may have very little to do with who we really are.[1]

—Gerald May

So, today I've been thinking about becoming more honest.

I've been thinking about it because I'm in Kansas City for a Women of Faith conference this weekend—the very same city where the gap that often exists between my behavior and my emotional reality became crystal-clear a year and a half ago. Prior to then, I would have admitted to struggling with lots of issues: I tend to be a people-pleaser, I talk too much, and I usually eat too many carbohydrates or buy expensive shoes when I'm sad. But I would not have described myself as *a liar*. Unless someone asks how much I weigh, I don't think of myself as the dishonest type. At least I didn't used to, until I ran onstage in Kansas City at a Women of Faith conference eighteen months ago to perform a rhythmically challenged rendition of Beyoncé's famous "Single Ladies" routine (minus the pelvic-thrusting parts).

I'd been practicing the routine for weeks. Even though it was just a silly introduction—a way to help the audience relax and let their hair down, since I was the first speaker—and only forty seconds in length, I still worked with a choreographer in Nashville to master some dance steps. I knew no one would be fooled into thinking I should try out for *So You Think You Can Dance*, but I didn't want the audience to be unduly scarred either. Of course, it was a little unsettling when, after watching me for a few minutes in our first session, the choreographer said, "You have very good rhythm in your *upper body* . . . it's probably best to shift people's attention away from your lower body." However, after our third muscle-straining dance class, he pronounced me a much improved pupil and more than ready for my Kansas City debut.

Therefore, when I walked on the stage less than a week later, the "Single Ladies" song began playing, and thousands of women stood up and began bouncing to the beat, I was feeling relatively calm. That is until I pranced into "ready position" directly in front of one of the cameras and my mind went completely blank. I just stood there frozen like a deer in blinding halogen headlights. Somewhere deep in my paralyzed brain the thought occurred to me, *People are staring and music is thumping and I'm supposed to be dancing*, but I couldn't remember the first step to save my life. After a long awkward pause, I began to gyrate. Since I couldn't remember the moves I'd paid three hundred dollars a session for, I just wiggled everything I could really fast. It wasn't synchronized with the beat and it definitely wasn't pretty but at least my feet weren't glued to the floor anymore.

A few seconds into this most unfortunate routine I thought, *Okay, I feel like a complete idiot, but women are laughing hysterically. They must think this is physical comedy. They don't realize my mind is a scary black hole and I've forgotten my name.* Moments later, one of my tortoise shell pumps went flying across the stage followed by the tacky gob of rubber that kept the shoe from chafing my heel. Of course, I didn't mean to kick it off, because that left me with just one four-inch heel to clomp around on, but that only seemed to make the audience hoot more. By the time the music ended, I was wet with perspiration and completely dry-mouthed with residual panic. I tried to take a sip of water from the tiny cup on a stool by the edge of the stage before launching into my talk but my hands were shaking so badly I sloshed most of it on my outfit while trying to raise the cup to my lips.

I don't know if you've ever been a clomping, cotton-mouthed, vibrating ball of nerves, but if you have, you can understand why I marched into my counselor's office when I returned home to Nashville and said, *"Help!"* After flopping on her couch and describing my meltdown onstage, I asked Lynn what she thought was going on. Had someone pressed my "nutter" button? Was I allergic to boogying in front of people? Did I need to update my résumé, since Bible teachers who discombobulate in public aren't in high demand these days? She wisely explained that I was actually experiencing God's divine healing.

Lynn went on to remind me how I've been able to perform acceptably, whether in school or at church or in the workplace, when my emotions were a mess. How I often just put on a happy face and went through the motions, cramming what I considered to be "bad" or "weak" feelings into a closet to deal with later. When I was a little girl trying to navigate the minefield of my parents' acrimonious divorce and my own sexual molestation, shoving my heart into a closet to protect it was a survival skill. But now that I've grown up, that survival skill has morphed into a less-than-honest boulder that trips me up on the path of intimacy with God and with other people. My counselor said the meltdown was symbolic of how our heavenly Father wasn't letting me get away with dancing around as if I were okay when my heart was off-kilter. He loves me too much to continue allowing me to stuff my "stuff."

It's pretty easy to spot it when a gap exists between someone else's behavior and their emotional reality (I've learned it's a dead giveaway if a boyfriend is kissing you while stealing glances at the football game taking place on the television screen behind your head), but it's a whole lot harder to stare at the ripples in our own souls and wonder what's beneath the surfaces, much less to actually deal with the pain or shame or sadness that often exists at our very cores. Thankfully, our Savior doesn't just hold up a mirror;

He also holds our hands while we gaze into it. And He won't let go, even if we have sweaty palms.

We can become more honest by clinging to Christ while cleaning out the closets of our souls.

How Jesus Helps Us Become More Honest

Jesus continued: "There was a man who had two sons. The younger one said to his father, 'Father, give me my share of the estate.' So he divided his property between them.

"Not long after that, the younger son got together all he had, set off for a distant country and there squandered his wealth in wild living. After he had spent everything, there was a severe famine in that whole country, and he began to be in need. So he went and hired himself out to a citizen of that country, who sent him to his fields to feed pigs. He longed to fill his stomach with the pods that the pigs were eating, but no one gave him anything.

"When he came to his senses, he said, 'How many of my father's hired men have food to spare, and here I am starving to death! I will set out and go back to my father and say to him: Father, I have sinned against heaven and against you. I am no longer worthy to be called your son; make me like one of your hired men.' So he got up and went to his father.

"But while he was still a long way off, his father saw

him and was filled with compassion for him; he ran to his son, threw his arms around him and kissed him.

"The son said to him, 'Father, I have sinned against heaven and against you. I am no longer worthy to be called your son.'

"But the father said to his servants, 'Quick! Bring the best robe and put it on him. Put a ring on his finger and sandals on his feet. Bring the fattened calf and kill it. Let's have a feast and celebrate. For this son of mine was dead and is alive again; he was lost and is found.' So they began to celebrate.

"Meanwhile, the older son was in the field. When he came near the house, he heard music and dancing. So he called one of the servants and asked him what was going on. 'Your brother has come,' he replied, 'and your father has killed the fattened calf because he has him back safe and sound.'

"The older brother became angry and refused to go in. So his father went out and pleaded with him. But he answered his father, 'Look! All these years I've been slaving for you and never disobeyed your orders. Yet you never gave me even a young goat so I could celebrate with my friends. But when this son of yours who has squandered your property with prostitutes comes home, you kill the fattened calf for him!'

"'My son,' the father said, 'you are always with me, and everything I have is yours. But we had to celebrate and be glad, because this brother of yours was dead and is alive again; he was lost and is found.'" (Luke 15:11–32)

The Heart of His Story

I think this familiar parable is a wonderful "mirror passage" that can help us look at what's really going on in our inner beings. However, it's crucial to remember the historical context in order to grasp how it applies to our own *stuff*. According to the beginning of Luke 15, there were two distinct groups of people listening to Jesus tell this story: the first was a crowd of "tax-collectors and sinners"—men and women who had swindled and partied and gyrated along with numerous other moral mistakes. Then there were the "Pharisees and the teachers of the law"—folks who lived fastidiously according to the Holy Scriptures, who were careful not to make any public moral missteps (Luke 15:1). Obviously, the wayward hellions identified with the rebellious younger brother in the parable, and the law-abiding listeners identified with the sanctimonious elder brother.

While the traditional application of this passage has been the divine forgiveness available to repentant prodigals, I agree with author and pastor Tim Keller's more atypical assessment: "The targets of this story are not the 'wayward sinners' but religious people who do everything the Bible requires. . . . It is a mistake, then, to think Jesus tells this story primarily to assure younger brothers of his unconditional love."[2]

Keller went on to say, "Jesus' purpose is not to warm our hearts but to shatter our categories."[3] In other words, this isn't one of those sermons to download so we can forward it on to spiritually errant friends or relatives. It's one we need to marinate in ourselves. And I can tell you that when I soaked in this story, lots of impurities began bobbing to my surface. Junk began spilling off the shelves of my overpacked emotional closet.

I realized that, just as the elder brother tried to protect his "rights" by moralistic behavior, I've tried to protect myself from feeling pain or sadness by pasting on a happy face and pretending everything was all right when it wasn't. Even more significantly, I need to repent not just of my "bad things," such as gossiping, using expletives in traffic, and the like, but also for the *unrighteous reasons* behind why I often do my "good things." It struck me that, if I really believe our Savior came into this world to redeem broken people, I have to trust Jesus enough to race toward Him, knowing all my junk might just be flapping in the wind for all the world to see.

Hope for Our Ongoing Stories

My friend Nicole Johnson is a brilliant actor and writer. She wrote a piece for Women of Faith this year that includes the poignant and profound line: "We keep our secrets, and then our secrets keep us." That is essentially the lesson God has been teaching me over and over again for the past year and a half—hiding my feelings makes me heartsick.

Furthermore, His arms are a safe place to discombobulate. We don't have to have it all together in His presence. We can trust Him not to raise His eyebrows in disapproval at the mess that appears when we open the closet doors of our souls. He won't turn up His nose in disgust at the musty smell that seeps out. Instead, our Redeemer will carefully help us sort the treasures from the trash. If we'll just be honest about the emotional boxes we've squirreled away, Jesus will take charge of the cleaning process.

Living in Light of His Story

Dear Jesus, thank You so much for Your promise to be close to the brokenhearted and near to those whose lives are crushed. Help me to remember Your proximity and process all my feelings with You instead of shoving select ones into the recesses of my soul, where, like shards of unremoved glass, they'll eventually cause infection. Amen.

Personal Reflection and/or Group Discussion Questions

1. What's the biggest lie you remember being caught in when you were little? What were the consequences of getting caught?

2. In which of these three situations would you be more likely to be dishonest: to avoid conflict/keep the peace; to make yourself look more attractive and fit in with a particular group; or to keep from hurting someone else's feelings?

3. Do you think there are any "righteous" reasons that legitimize dishonesty?

4. Reread the story of the prodigal son in Luke 15. Which of the two brothers do you most identify with in this season of your life? Please explain your answer.

5. How would you describe the correlation between a *sense of entitlement* and *dishonesty*?

6. When has telling the truth—better yet, *living* the truth—resulted in an elevated pulse and sweaty palms for you?

7. Read Psalm 101. If you had to write a chorus for this Old Testament "song," what would the lyrics be?

Journal Entry

Please consider completing this sentence in your personal journal:

    So, today I've been thinking about how I can be more authentic, Jesus, and . . .

chapter 13
PUTTING DOWN THE PEN

I had always felt life first as a story: and if there is a story there is a storyteller.[1]

—G. K. Chesterton

So, today I've been thinking about becoming more content.

In other words, I'm ruminating about what it would look like to be completely satisfied in Christ, regardless of what's going on in my life. These thoughts were stirred by an innocent question my primary care doctor asked during a routine physical a few days ago. Just as he was placing the cold metal disc of a stethoscope on my chest, he asked, "Are you still single?"

I've known this doctor for years; we used to attend the

same church and his wife and I have been in several Bible studies together. Therefore, he wasn't being inappropriate, and he definitely isn't some V-necked-shiny-shirt-wearing Casanova with an ulterior motive; he was just being polite. But my guess is he still detected a slight wobble in my heart after he kindly asked that question.

Never in a million years would I have guessed I'd be approaching fifty without a husband. My mom has been married twice; my Dad Harper has been married three times; both of my siblings have made at least one trip down the aisle; and the majority of my girlfriends have worn something borrowed and something blue. Until recently, I assumed I would too.

Now I'm not one of those girls who started compiling a "My Future Wedding" scrapbook in high school. Nor did I put off buying dishes and towels after college so as to safeguard the inevitable joy I'd feel when receiving those items as gifts at some distant bridal shower—one of my former roommates actually used that as an excuse when we invited her to join us on a Target run where they were having a big home goods sale, and she wasn't even dating anyone at the time!—but I still thought having a man look directly into my eyes and proclaim "I do" while sliding a ring on my left hand would be part of my story.

I also didn't dream I'd end up childless. From the time I was a little girl, I thought I'd have my own babies. Preferably three or four. Unlike some of my more squeamish friends, the thought of "pulling a basketball out of a nostril" (as I've heard childbirth described) never bothered me. Neither did the thought of dirty diapers or sleep deprivation. I sincerely believed that wonderful talcum-powder scent would intoxicate me to the point that the inconveniences that come with a tiny human would be undetectable, or at least insignificant. Compared to the toothless grin and chubby thighs of an infant, what's the big deal about a little poo or dark circles under your eyes? And don't even get me started about those precious clay handprints toddlers make their mommies in preschool. Good night, I'd take out a second mortgage for one of those!

However, a sweetheart who leaves wet towels on the floor and a minivan full of kids and soccer balls hasn't been written into my story. There aren't any whiskers in my bathroom sink or miniature muddy cleats by my door. It's just me. Sure, I put up a tree at Christmas and pile presents for close friends and their children underneath it, but oh how I wish there were gifts for my own kids under there. What I wouldn't give to be able to hang stockings monogrammed with *my* children's names on the mantel. And while I enjoy flying to Florida to surprise my mom on Mother's Day, sometimes there's a hollow ache in my spirit afterward when I realize no one will ever surprise me with a "Happy Mama's Day" visit or phone call.

If I had control of the pen, I would have written my life differently. I would have added a mate to fuss at and snuggle up to and grow old with. I would have inserted children to read to and cook for and defend in the principal's office. I'd have colored in a real family sitting around the table at Thanksgiving, instead of a group of dear single and divorced friends.

But I am not the author of my own life; God is. And the older I get, the more convinced I am that He's the perfect storyteller. When I reread chapters from my twenties (a season of tight skin and hair that wasn't chemically dependent), I can't help but notice how He protected me from two or three abusive guys with whom I almost paired. And how He protected some godly suitors from the vacuum of my then very-damaged heart. When I review my thirties and forties, I keep coming upon highlighted passages illustrating how week after week and month after month I get to travel around the country and experience the miracle of praying with people who are putting their hope in Jesus for the first time. That would be pretty hard to do if I were driving carpool every afternoon.

I am stingy when it comes to handing God the pen. Sometimes He has to pry my fingers loose, but with each new page of my story, I'm learning to trust His narrative more. I'm learning to believe in an ultimate happy ending, even when I don't like some of the chapters He writes, because as Paul reminds us in Romans: "And we know that in all things God works for the good of those who love him, who have been called according to his purpose" (Romans 8:28). And the psalmist eloquently sang, "As for me, I shall behold your face in righteousness; / when I awake, I shall be satisfied with your likeness" (Psalm 17:15 ESV).

We can become more content by giving God the sole authorship of our biographies.

How Jesus Helps Us Become More Content

"Then the kingdom of heaven will be like ten virgins who took their lamps and went to meet the bridegroom. Five of them were foolish, and five were wise. For when the foolish took their lamps, they took no oil with them, but the wise took flasks of oil with their lamps. As the bridegroom was delayed, they all became drowsy and slept.

But at midnight there was a cry, 'Here is the bridegroom! Come out to meet him.' Then all those virgins rose and trimmed their lamps. And the foolish said to the wise, 'Give us some of your oil, for our lamps are going out.' But the wise answered, saying, 'Since there will not be enough for us and for you, go rather to the dealers and buy for yourselves.'

And while they were going to buy, the bridegroom came, and those who were ready went in with him to the marriage feast, and the door was shut. Afterward the other virgins came also, saying, 'Lord, lord, open to us.' But he answered, 'Truly, I say to you, I do not know you.' Watch therefore, for you know neither the day nor the hour." (Matthew 25:1–14 ESV)

The Heart of His Story

Craig Blomberg, a modern-day expert on parabolic literature, explains there were three main themes in the stories Jesus told: the graciousness of God, the demands of discipleship, and the dangers of disobedience. Blomberg goes on to explain that along with the sober effect they had on listeners, "Jesus' parables leave no neutral ground for casual interest or idle curiosity. They sharply divided their original audiences into disciples and opponents."[2] Oh how I'd love to know the ways in which this particular story impacted all the middle-aged, single girls in His original audience that day!

Of course, if they were at all familiar with the Torah (the Jewish Bible, essentially what we now refer to as the Old Testament), they knew God often used weddings and marriage to symbolize larger spiritual truths. I'm sure they had some meddling aunts or nosy neighbors who had perkily quoted Isaiah 54:5, "For thy Maker is thine husband; the LORD of hosts is his name" (KJV), after inquiring about whether they'd had any good dates recently. But I hope those single girls had more than a cognitive understanding of God as their heavenly Husband. I really hope they identified with the five wise chicks in Jesus' parable, the ones who were living in light of the promise of a perfect wedding day.

The best description I've found of the parallels between an ancient engaged Jewish couple and the relationship Christians now have with our Redeemer is in Alan Wright's book *Lover of My Soul*:

> Betrothed couples could have a lot of fun preparing for marriage. They could share their lives deeply. But there were limits to their intimacy. They belonged to each other, but they didn't wake up daily face to face. Totally

committed but not totally united. Plenty to celebrate but still preparing for the real party. Already husband and wife but not yet married. That's the picture of betrothal. And that's the beautiful picture of a Christian on earth. God the Father sent His Spirit into the world to seek a match for His only Son. He noticed you. It was love at first sight. His attraction fell upon you. He wooed you, enticed you, allured you. He paid an enormous bride price at a place called Golgotha. And when you consented to His betrothal agreement, you became His bride—His betrothed. The witness of His Spirit sealed the betrothal agreement. Nothing can break it. You're His. He is yours. Rightly you can be called the wife of this heavenly Husband. All the benefits of the marriage relationship are promised to you. But something better awaits. You've plenty to celebrate during your betrothal, but the real wedding party is yet to come.[3]

Pastor Wright also described how a Jewish bridegroom would go back to his father's house to prepare a new place for them to live together. He would typically labor for a year, sometimes even longer, constructing an annex or upper room on the home in which he grew up. Or, if he were wealthy, the husband-to-be would build a brand-spanking-new house for his bride-to-be. However, she didn't get to make runs to Home Depot with her beloved, because tradition compelled her to stay behind with her family, often in a village many miles away. And it was not until the groom's dad inspected the finished quarters and officially declared the new room or home to be satisfactory for the young couple to reside in that the bridegroom raced back to retrieve his bride. Then, when the news of his impending return reached her neighborhood, people lit lanterns and danced in the streets to celebrate. I'm guessing the lights were brighter and they boogied harder if the bride was considerably older than most!

Hope for Our Ongoing Stories

If you've put your faith in Jesus Christ, you can enjoy deep contentment. We can bask and revel in the reality that we have been completely accepted and are totally adored by the Son of God. We can pick the petals off daisies and say dreamily, "He loves me" with the absolute assurance that "He loves me not" will never, ever apply to us again. But to be content in Christ's affection isn't the same thing as being complacent. We aren't just hoping for something that may not happen. We aren't buying *Brides* magazine on the off-chance that we'll snag a man. The dress isn't going to stay in the closet sealed in plastic because we are officially engaged to the King of kings and Lord of lords. We've been bought with the most costly dowry ever paid. And though this season of betrothal is stretching longer than some of us would like, a wedding more wonderful than we can possibly imagine really is right around the corner. Therefore, may we seek to be content in the *already*, sighing as we admire the sparkling rock Jesus slid onto our finger, but conscious of the *not yet*. Satisfied with our salvation but still eagerly awaiting consummation.

Living in Light of His Story

Dear Jesus, I can't believe You picked me! And I can't wait to ride off in a limo trailing soup cans with You! Please help me to rest in Your love yet also look forward to the wedding party Your friend John described. Amen.

Personal Reflection and/or Group Discussion Questions

1. What chapters of your life story are *vastly different* from the way you thought they would look when you were younger?

2. Looking back over your story now, what particular chapter stands out as one that seemed tragic when it happened but actually produced great treasure?

3. Read Romans 8:18–28. What context does the whole passage bring to the single verse of Romans 8:28?

4. Read 2 Peter 3:8–9. In what relationship or circumstance of your life does God *seem* slow in keeping His promises?

5. Read Romans 5:1–5. How would you summarize the connection between suffering and hope? Between hope and contentment?

6. If your life story were being filmed as a movie, what do you think the title would be? What actress would you like to see play you?

Journal Entry

Please consider completing this sentence in your personal journal:

So, today I've been thinking about putting down my pen and becoming more content with You as the author of my life, Jesus, and . . .

chapter 14
CARRYING HOME A GIANT

Grace means you're in a different universe from where you had been stuck, when you had absolutely no way to get there on your own. [1]

—Anne Lamott

So, today I've been thinking about becoming more dependent on God.

Right now I don't have another choice. I'm sitting in the Nashville airport waiting to board a flight to Orlando in the hopes that I'll make it home before Dad Angel dies. Mom just called to see if I can get there any faster, because the hospice nurse told her his death is imminent. But I can't make these laughing families on their way to Disney move down the Jetway any quicker. I can't make the flight attendant skip the safety speech. And I don't think the pilots will break any FAA speed rules on the way to Florida on my behalf. I'm at the liberty of "life goes on as usual no matter what's going on in your world." So I just have to sit here and pray God will allow me to make it home to see Dad one last time before his soul leaves his tired body.

I'm overwhelmed and anxious. I feel as if I'm going to throw up, and my chest physically hurts, as if my heart's ripping apart at the seams. When I asked the gate agent if I could board early to get a seat near the front of the plane so I could depart as fast as possible when we land, he asked why. I calmly explained that my father is dying and I was trying to get to his bedside before he did. Then I burst into tears. I feel like I'm holding on by a thread as tenuous as spider's silk.

All I can do is breathe deeply, focusing on inhaling God's peace and exhaling anxiety, as my counselor taught me to do in times of extreme stress, and recite the memory verses that have flooded my mind: "My grace is sufficient for you, for my power is made perfect in weakness" (2 Corinthians 12:9); "Thou wilt keep him in perfect peace, whose mind is stayed on thee" (Isaiah 26:3 KJV); and "The LORD is close to the broken hearted and saves those who are crushed in spirit" (Psalm 34:18). During this agonizing wait, I have to believe the Good Shepherd is leading me step by step. Otherwise, I'm afraid I'm going to fall.

I wrote those beginning paragraphs exactly a week ago today. Much has happened since last Monday. By the grace of God,

I made it home just before Dad slipped into a mostly unconscious state. The last time he sat up in bed on his own was to hold out his arms for me. When I knelt down, he looked directly into my eyes and said weakly, "I love you, Lisa," and held me while I sobbed into his chest. I can't begin to explain how much I needed that kind of tender closure with him. We spent the next two days and nights sitting or lying beside his bed (he'd made clear his intentions about dying at home instead of in a hospital), holding his hands, telling him stories, and singing worship songs. I teased that my off-key singing would probably quicken his steps toward heaven.

The last twenty-four hours were especially rough. Since Dad Angel had suffered with Alzheimer's for years, we thought we were prepared for his death, but we weren't prepared for him to die the way he did. It wasn't at all the way I've seen it depicted in the movies. There were no violins playing in the background. Shafts of white light didn't illuminate the room. It was sad and wretched and miserable. Whenever we had to move him or change him, he'd open his eyes and moan. Then he'd try to talk but couldn't. Sometimes he looked really scared. He didn't want to die.

My little brother, John Price; Mom; and I took shifts throughout the night so someone would be with him every second while the other two tried to take short naps. Sometime after midnight on Tuesday, after the hospice nurse checked his vital signs and said Dad might last another week, I finally took an Ambien to try and sleep a little longer since I hadn't slept more than thirty minutes at a stretch since Saturday night. Typically an Ambien knocks me out for seven or eight hours straight. Instead, I woke with a start—almost as if someone had splashed cold water in my face—at 5:15 a.m. I hurried downstairs to find everyone asleep, but I noticed Dad's breathing had gotten much worse. So I woke up Mom, and we took over while John Price went into the next room.

At six o'clock I said, "Mama, Dad's dying."

She asked if I thought she should go get my brother, and I said yes. A few minutes later, with Mom holding Dad's left hand, me holding his right, and J.P. holding his head, Dad died. Thankfully, the very end was very peaceful.

The next twelve hours were anything but peaceful. It took almost an hour for the funeral home van to get to our house. When I opened the door, I was shocked to find a kind but flustered heavyset elderly man and an elderly woman with a hearing aid standing there wringing their hands. Of course, I was expecting two strong men instead of this frail couple, and I immediately wondered, *How in the world are they going to be able to carry Dad's body down that big staircase on the front of the house?* Although Dad had lost a lot of weight in the last few months of his life, he was still at least 150 pounds. I won't go into details, but suffice it to say that John Price and I had to help load our father's body on a gurney, then carry him through the house and down two flights of stairs to the driveway, or else wait another hour for younger, stronger replacements.

My truck-driving, deer-hunting brother is one of the toughest guys I know, but out of all the kids, he was the closest to Dad, so that heart-wrenching march took all the emotional strength J.P. had. After watching the van slowly drive away, he took off for a walk in the woods (my parents live in a rural, riverside community in Central Florida surrounded by forest and wetlands), and I went back inside to check on Mom. I don't know if you've ever had the heavy privilege of being with someone during their darkest moments of mourning, but I can tell you it will leave a deep gash of empathy on your soul.

Twenty minutes after the funeral home van left, four other vehicles rolled in to fill the gap. I was beyond grateful to see Jeanette, Susan, Darlene, and Clayton—Mom's three sisters and one of her brothers-in-law. After long hugs, a precious time of prayer, and a short discussion, we agreed on a course of action. And what happened next was like one of those Amish barn raisings I've seen on the Discovery Channel. Within an hour, we had Dad's bedroom completely cleaned and everything that was no longer needed, including his bed frame and mattress, packed into the back of Clayton's truck for disposal, so Mom wouldn't have to deal with it.

Then Darlene and I went to the funeral home to take care of the details for a next-day burial (as per Mom and Dad's wishes). Even though everything was already paid for, it still took almost three hours to get the official stuff signed and settled. During that time frame, insulation from the ceiling of the world's tackiest and most inept funeral home fell onto my head and into my lap; we were subject to the shameless hawking of memorial knick-knacks; I was treated like someone who clubs baby seals for a living after refusing an expensive coffin upgrade; and a disagreement broke out between the funeral home director and the cemetery representative regarding Dad's exact burial plot location. After listening to their verbal sparring go on and on, I finally walked into the director's office and showed her where north and south were on the cemetery map key so they could agree where to dig Dad's grave and place the vault.

By the time I got back to my mom's house, I was so dog-tired I could barely keep my eyes open. However, it was still hard to fall asleep, knowing Mom and I were alone in the house. It was oddly quiet without the rhythmic whooshing of Dad's oxygen machine and the hum of the dryer heating up the blankets Mom kept rotating for him. I found myself lying in bed, staring at the ceiling, reciting the same memory verses I had said in the airport only three days earlier: "My grace is sufficient for you, for my power is made perfect in weakness" . . . "Thou wilt keep him in perfect peace, whose mind is stayed on thee" . . . "The LORD is close to the broken hearted and saves those who are crushed in spirit."

We woke up to a sunny, cool Thursday—the kind of day Dad always said was perfect for spending on the St. Johns River. We had a simple graveside service for him at ten o'clock. Mom said he didn't want a formal funeral, so his family and a few old fishing buddies just gathered together and told stories about him. We didn't make him sound nobler than he was. We didn't pretend he was a flaw-less husband, father, or stepfather. We just talked about what we loved most about him and what we'd miss now that he was gone. And then we pondered how God was finally able to convince John Gordon Angel that He loved him. I confessed I'd stopped praying for Dad to believe in Jesus. After forty years of seemingly unanswered prayers, I'd all but given up hope. But our Redeemer is amazingly patient and tenacious. He pursued Dad Angel with goodness and mercy until he finally succumbed to the gospel, just eight weeks before he died.

I know beyond a shadow of a doubt that God carried that giant of a man all the way home, which was no small miracle. It has widened my eyes further to the power of divine grace. It has convinced me that I can depend on my heavenly Father to hold me up, even when my heart is failing and my knees are weak.

We can become more dependent on God by trusting Him with the full weight of our lives.

How Jesus Helps Us Become More Dependent

Jesus and his followers went to a place called Gethsemane. He said to them, "Sit here while I pray." Jesus took Peter, James, and John with him, and he began to be very sad and troubled. He said to them, "My heart is full of sorrow, to the point of death. Stay here and watch."

After walking a little farther away from them, Jesus fell to the ground and prayed that, if possible, he would not have this time of suffering. He prayed, "Abba, Father! You can do all things. Take away this cup of suffering. But do what you want, not what I want."

Then Jesus went back to his followers and found them asleep. He said to Peter, "Simon, are you sleeping? Couldn't you stay awake with me for one hour? Stay awake and pray for strength against temptation. The spirit wants to do what is right, but the body is weak."

Again Jesus went away and prayed the same thing. Then he went back to his followers, and again he found them asleep, because their eyes were very heavy. And they did not know what to say to him.

After Jesus prayed a third time, he went back to his followers and said to them, "Are you still sleeping and resting? That's enough. The time has come for the Son of Man to be handed over to sinful people. Get up, we must go. Look, here comes the man who has turned against me." (Mark 14:32–42 NCV)

The Heart of His Story

Jesus was desperate in the Garden of Gethsemane. He had the stooped shoulders and bloodshot eyes of a man in agony. In Matthew's account of what took place during those dark hours in that olive grove, it says Jesus was so troubled He told the disciples, "My heart is full of sorrow, to the point of death" (Matthew 26:38 NCV), and Dr. Luke adds the medical note that the Messiah was under such extreme stress that "His sweat was like drops of blood falling to the ground" (Luke 22:44 NCV). Contrary to some sermons, Jesus didn't square His shoulders and face the cross with unblinking fortitude. He wasn't a stoic martyr; He experienced distress. Not because He was afraid of death, but because He dreaded being separated from His Father and receiving His wrath. But He endured that unimaginable ache alone.

Even mouthy, well-intentioned Peter, who'd vowed to stick to Jesus like Velcro, fell asleep while the Messiah mourned under those gnarled trees. Our Savior was bereft of companionship. No one dropped by with a pint of chicken soup. No one wrote Him a note expressing his or her condolences. Every single person abandoned Him during His time of deepest need. And that's why the author of Hebrews was able to preach, "God is the One who made all things, and all things are for his glory. He wanted to have many children share his glory, so he made the One who leads people to salvation perfect through suffering. . . . And now he can help those who are tempted, because he himself suffered and was tempted" (Hebrews 2:10, 18 NCV). Jesus didn't supernaturally skip to the front of the pain line. He chose instead to be an empathetic Hero, sharing perfectly in the frailty and loneliness of our humanity.

C. S. Lewis described this miracle of divine empathy much more eloquently than I can: "But supposing God became a man—suppose our human nature which can suffer and die was amalgamated with God's nature in one person—then that person could help us . . . That is the sense in which He pays our debt, and suffers for us what He Himself need not suffer at all."[2] Hallelujah! What an undeservedly compassionate Savior.

Mark goes on to explain that Jesus didn't set our weight

down after Gethsemane either. He continued to carry mankind's shame and grief and depravity up a hill on the west side of the city of Jerusalem called Golgotha. Then He adjusted the load of us on His back before climbing onto a cross and submitting to humiliating torture. Toward the end of His crucifixion, just before He died, Jesus cried out, "My God, my God, why have you rejected me?" (Mark 15:34 NCV). It's the only time in Scripture that Jesus is recorded as using God's formal title instead of addressing Him as "Father." Why? Because it's the only time His Dad *despised* him.

Jesus didn't live an easy life or die an easy death. The glory of Easter was preceded by the sorrow of absolute rejection. Our Redeemer knows what it feels like to be stripped of all comfort and ease. He experienced the betrayal of best friends. He sobbed alone, without a single person offering support. Yet, instead of trying to drown His sorrows with a margarita or spilling His guts to a sympathetic stranger on a plane, He endured. He shouldered the greatest possible anguish, being completely abandoned by everyone including God, so we would never have to carry that burden ourselves.

Hope for Our Ongoing Stories

I didn't used to believe Jesus was enough for me. I probably wouldn't have said it out loud, though. It's certainly not what I wrote in seminary papers or taught at Christian women's conferences. But somewhere in the recesses of my heart and mind, I was afraid that if the people I loved most abandoned me, I would die. I cognitively subscribed to Blaise Pascal's theological assertion: "There is a God-shaped vacuum in the heart of every person, and it can never be filled by any created thing. It can only be filled by God, made known through Jesus Christ." But in reality I was an emotional colander, always hoping some human could plug the holes in my soul.

It wasn't until I hit the bottom I was terrified of this past year that I found the love of Christ really is enough to sustain me, no matter what. Buckling under the weight of my own life is what helped me fall into the arms of God. I didn't just stumble into His grace; I collapsed there in a messy heap! And you know what? It's by far the best thing that's ever happened to me.

Living in Light of His Story

Dear Jesus, thank You for promising that Your grace is all we need and that Your power works best in weakness. Please help me trust in Your compassionate strength and remember my own frailties, so I won't be tempted to try and lug heavy stuff by myself anymore. I'd rather stay right here at Your feet, totally dependent on You. Amen.

Personal Reflection and/or Group Discussion Questions

1. What is the thing and/or relationship you're most afraid of losing?

2. What would you describe as your greatest loss in the past few years?

3. How has the grief over that loss affected your relationship with God?

4. In her wonderful devotional *Jesus Calling*, Sarah Young wrote, "Rehearsing your troubles results in experiencing them many times, whereas you are meant to go through them only when they actually occur."[3] What does "rehearsing your troubles" look like through the lens of your personality?

5. Read Matthew 11:28–30. What would it look like for you to truly collapse into the caring arms of God?

6. Who specifically would you need to depend on less in order to depend on God completely?

7. Read 1 Peter 5:7. Given the fact that *casting* is a verb, what action could you do today to become more reliant on God?

8. Read Joshua 1:5–9. Describe two specific places you need to be reminded that God is going with you this week.

Journal Entry

Please consider completing this sentence in your personal journal:

So, today I've been thinking about becoming absolutely devoted to and dependent on You, Jesus, and . . .

chapter 15
THE GALVANIZING EFFECT
OF GRATITUDE

*A stunned and grateful heart is free to love because it has been
captured with the hilarious paradox that we are unlovely but loved,
and unable to love but free to try without condemnation. And all
efforts to love are made lovely and useful by a great Lover who
superintends all our bumbling efforts and turns the dross of mixed
motives to the gold of eternal intentions.*[1]

—Dr. Dan Allender and Dr. Tremper Longman

So, today I've been thinking about becoming more
grateful.

Which is apropos since today is Thanksgiving. I've
always loved this particular holiday. I love the crazed

grocery store runs late the night before when we realize we need more rolls or forgot to get marshmallows for the sweet potato casserole. I love peeling a bushel of navel oranges for our family's traditional citrus-heavy ambrosia. I love gathering around a table with people I care about, holding hands, and bowing our heads to pray together. I love listening to the multiple conversations that flow between cousins and siblings and friends the way water runs over rocks in a stream. And of course, I love the eating-copious-amounts-of-yummy-food-until-I-have-to-unbutton-my-pants-or-they're-going-to-cut-off-my-circulation part!

The only time I can remember not loving a Thanksgiving season was in 1979. I was a junior in high school and had been briefly brainwashed by an articulate history teacher, who was both vehemently agnostic and anti-American in her sentiments. She had spent the better part of the fall burying bombs in our sixteen-year-old belief systems and then detonating them with fiery speeches on such subjects as the crass consumerism that built our national economy, the federal conspiracy that led to the Cuban Missile Crisis, and the moral superiority of socialism. Looking back, I can't believe our class swallowed her skewed rhetoric. I guess most teenagers just aren't savvy enough to know they're being sold sociopolitical swampland. But my mom sure was.

A few days before Turkey Day that year, we were in the kitchen when I cheekily announced something along the lines of, "I'm no longer a fan of Thanksgiving, because it is a self-congratulatory display of American imperialism."

Mom was quiet for a moment. It's a wonder she didn't whack my big, idiotic head with a frying pan. Then she asked how I had come to that conclusion. I quickly summarized what we'd been learning in Advanced American History and how "Ms. Lefty" was teaching us about everything that's *wrong* with our country.

Mom replied, "Well, maybe Ms. Lefty should move to Siberia if she hates America so much!" She then got up on her own fervent soapbox and reminded me about all the things that are *right* about the land of the free and home of the brave.

Thirty years have passed and I can still remember most of Mom's talking points. She waxed poetic about how our country was founded by men and women who longed for freedom: Freedom to express their faith in God. Freedom to have a voice in how the place they called home should be governed. Freedom to enjoy the fruit of their chosen labor. And freedom from persecution, regardless of their race or creed. With an indignant hand on her hip and a spatula waving in the air for emphasis, Mom put that teacher's bitter bias in proper perspective. I'm the same age now as Mom was then and have formed a comparable opinion about our country. I still don't think it's flawless: I hate armed conflict and wish there was another viable option besides deadly force to defeat evil and terrorism. I think politicians should be accountable to stricter term limits. And I think people who peddle pornography for a living should be forced to share cramped, windowless apartments with camels who have irritable bowel syndrome.

But I firmly believe the blessings of the United States of America far outweigh its curses, and there's nowhere else on earth I'd rather live.

Furthermore, my mother's lesson has extended far beyond the confines of a national holiday. By teaching me to search for what is good, true, and noble, even when I have to dig around in a vat filled with some not-so-good, not-so-true, or not-so-noble things, Mom handed me the key to living a life saturated with gratitude. She taught me to appreciate God's beauty, even when it's decorated with thorns; to recognize the luxuries He generously affords us disguised as basic necessities; and to savor the sweet fruit from His garden, even though you might have to spit out a few seeds while eating it.

That's why I have the freedom to feel joy today, in spite of my lingering sorrow over Dad Angel's death. Last Thursday I was standing beside his casket, and this Thursday I had a turkey in the oven. Not a whole turkey, mind you, just a few slices. Because I missed so much work last week, I wasn't able to fly back to Florida this week for Thanksgiving. When I realized I had to stay in Nashville by myself, I decided to invite a divorced friend, whose father died of a heart attack last month, to join me. I knew she didn't really have anywhere to go this year either. So I set the table with my best plates and linen napkins and went to a gourmet grocery store and bought all the fixings. I have to admit that a long table set for only two does look a bit lopsided. We couldn't help teasing that our holiday "gathering" was more like Charlie Brown's Christmas tree, rather spindly and sparse. But then, in the spirit of the day, we started talking about everything we were thankful for, and before we knew it, we were laughing and interrupting each other with yet another story about how we'd been blessed.

After the dishes were washed and put away, and my guest was on her way home, I went for a trail run. I wore a fleece because it was cold and the lens of gratitude because I want to keep focusing on good things today. Instead of a deserted park, I discovered a peaceful sanctuary complete with a bird choir. Instead of forlorn, leafless trees, I admired how statuesque the oak and cedar sentinels guarding my work-out were. Instead of chubby thighs, I appreciated the sturdy stems that have propelled me through life without much complaint. As the trail stretched on, I pondered the water-shed events of the last six months: a little cancer, the loss of a friend, and the loss of Dad Angel. Then I began to sing the chorus of a new worship song that has been my musical anchor lately:

> I will say of the Lord he is my refuge
> I will say of the Lord he is my strength
> I will say of the Lord he is my shelter, my hiding place[2]

I can honestly say I'm grateful for how loneliness ulti-mately makes me long for heaven. I'm grateful the lesion above my ear turned out to be malignant, because it forced me to admit more of my weaknesses and ask the Good Shepherd for help. I'm even grateful for Dad's death, because knowing his life was coming to an end is what finally compelled him to find refuge in God. Most of all, I'm grateful that every stumbling step I take leads me further into the perfect love and grace of Jesus Christ.

We can become more grateful by searching for God's goodness and mercy in the oft-present ruins of everyday life.

How Jesus Helps Us Become More Grateful

> Now on his way to Jerusalem, Jesus traveled along the border between Samaria and Galilee. As he was going into a village, ten men who had leprosy met him. They stood at a distance and called out in a loud voice, "Jesus, Master, have pity on us!"
>
> When he saw them, he said, "Go, show yourselves to the priests." And as they went, they were cleansed.
>
> One of them, when he saw he was healed, came back, praising God in a loud voice. He threw himself at Jesus' feet and thanked him—and he was a Samaritan.
>
> Jesus asked, "Were not all ten cleansed? Where are the other nine? Has no one returned to give praise to God except this foreigner?" Then he said to him, "Rise and go; your faith has made you well." (Luke 17:11–19 UPDATED NIV)

The Heart of His Story

Jesus and His disciples were taking a road trip to Jerusalem along a route bordering the acrimonious regions of Samaria and Galilee. When their trek took them to a village, a group of ten guys began shouting at Him from across the street. Even from a distance Jesus could tell they were all lepers. Anyone could have because, according to Old Testament law, whoever was afflicted with leprosy—the oldest disease in recorded history[3]—had to wear torn clothes and unkempt hair when in public. They were also required to yell, "Unclean, unclean!" whenever anyone else got too close, so as to keep others from being infected with their terrible skin disease.[4] During the first century, when Jesus' earthly ministry took place, lepers were literally and figuratively quarantined. Cut off. Stigmatized. Stranded on their own hellish island without any social or physical contact with "well" people. And that only describes their emotional torment.

Author Ken Gire helped explain the physical anguish lepers endured:

> It's a horrible disease, leprosy. It begins with little specks on the eyelids and on the palms of the hand. Then it spreads over the body. It bleaches the hair white. It casts a cadaverous pallor over the skin, crusting it with scales and erupting over it with oozing sores.
>
> But that's just what happens on the surface. Penetrating the skin the disease, like a moth, eats its way through the network of nerves woven throughout the body's tissues. Soon the body becomes numb to the point of sensory deprivation, numbed to both pleasure and pain. A toe can break, and it will register no pain. And sensing no pain, the leper will continue walking,

only to worsen the break and hasten the infection. One by one the appendages of the leper suffer their fate against the hard edges of life.[5]

Dr. Paul Brand, one of the leading authorities on Hansen's disease (the modern medical name for leprosy) in the twentieth century, described how patients at a leprosarium in India would reach directly into a fire to retrieve something they'd accidentally dropped, walk barefoot across broken glass, and work their fingers literally down to the bone as a result of their extreme nerve damage. Worse still, he documented numerous cases of sleeping patients losing portions of their fingers and toes to hungry rats during the night, which led to the rule that everyone released from the hospital had to take home a cat for nocturnal protection.[6]

It's hard to imagine a more horrible affliction, and it's totally understandable why this motley crew of multinational lepers was desperate enough to yell, "Please have pity on us, Master!" at Jesus. Acknowledging Him as a teacher (the word *master* actually means "rabbi"—in other words, a Jewish sage or scholar), they can only hope He has the wisdom to help them. But it's a Hail Mary pass because ancient rabbis were not reputed to be professional healers. They were highly regarded for dispensing knowledge, not medical miracles.

And given Christ's response to their plea, "Go, show yourselves to the priests" (which was in adherence to Leviticus 14:1-32), at least a few of them probably dropped their heads and sighed, thinking, *We should have known this teacher dude would give some by-the-book response.* It definitely wasn't the answer they were wanting. They wanted a *cure*, not a class assignment. But for reasons Luke doesn't explain, they still obeyed Christ's command. Maybe it was the authoritative tone in His voice, or maybe they simply didn't have anything better to do, since there weren't any more strangers behind Jesus they could beg for help. So they turned to walk toward the rectory, and when they did, all ten men were completely and astonishingly healed.

I've witnessed the whoops and victory chants of friends who've been pronounced cancer-free after long bouts with that disease, and my guess is the men in this gospel story reacted with the same exuberant glee. They were probably jumping up and down and giving each other high-fives and hugging bystanders and doing cartwheels through the middle of town. Based on Luke's account, they had a riotous "we're healed" party but completely forgot to thank their Doctor. All except one. One lone former leper turned around and fell at the dusty feet of the Great Physician and said, "Thank You."

The only other detail we know about this guy who remembered his manners is that, unlike the others, he was a Samaritan. That means he suffered the social stigma and emotional torment of being considered dirty long before he became infected with leprosy.

Seven hundred fifty years before the time of Christ, a violent people group called the Assyrians conquered the northern kingdom of Israel where Samaria is located. This resulted in a country where Jews and Assyrians intermarried and produced a race that was half-Jewish and half-Assyrian, who came to be known as *Samaritans*. For centuries Jewish people vilified Samaritans as half-breed, impure traitors. In fact, their hatred was so intense that they cursed them publicly in the synagogue and prayed that God would exclude them from eternal life.

Thus, to say this poor fellow had a double whammy of hard life is a major understatement. He was from the ultimate wrong side of the tracks. He definitely didn't make the football team or have anyone to sit next to in the lunchroom. Regular pariahs wouldn't give him the time of day. I think he's the one who remembered to thank Jesus for restoring him because he's the one who remembered most how horrible being broken and outcast had been. He was especially grateful because he hadn't forgotten how completely disfigured his life was before the Messiah graciously entered it.

Hope for Our Ongoing Stories

Mom taught me that Thanksgiving is about remembering to focus on good things, even in the presence of bad things. This gospel tutorial on thanksgiving goes a step further. It illustrates how remembering bad things can actually bring divine goodness and mercy into sharper focus. In the context of being *lost*, being *found* is more wondrous. In the context of being *persecuted*, finding *acceptance* is more precious. In the context of being *sick*, being *healed* is more miraculous. So I don't want to forget all the mistake chapters in my story, such as when I ran away from home during a teenage tantrum and got pneumonia after being foolish enough to pout outside during a thunderstorm. Or when I ran away from my senses a few years later and into the arms of a young man who only wanted one thing from me, and it certainly wasn't my undying love. Or when I stopped praying for my stepfather to come to faith in Christ, because he could be so difficult that I wasn't sure grace was big enough to include him. Apart from Jesus, I'm a faithless prodigal waiting to happen. But I'm learning that the roots of gratitude grow deepest in the sober soil of remembering how hopeless my life is without God.

Living in Light of His Story

Oh Jesus, help me to never forget the lack of peace I had during especially sinful seasons. How lonely I've been when I haven't sought refuge in You. How jarring and discordant life is without Your voice. I'm so grateful You continually rescue me from the disease of my own rebellion. You have restored me into a living hope. I look forward to the day I can lie at Your nail-scarred feet and say thank You. Amen.

Personal Reflection and/or Group Discussion Questions

1. Describe the top three things (not individuals) you're thankful for today.

2. Who are three people you're especially grateful for this season?

3. Read Psalms 34 and 107. Both of these psalms are classified as "thanksgiving psalms," and most thanksgiving psalms include gratitude for a specific calamity from which God rescued the psalmist (e.g., a close call in battle, literal captivity). What "calamity" has God rescued you from recently?

4. In light of the assertion about the leper being "especially grateful because he hadn't forgotten how completely disfigured his life was before the Messiah graciously entered it," how would you describe the disfigurement in your life before you met Jesus?

5. Read Philippians 4:6–7. What are some practical ways you've found to approach God with gratitude on really bad days?

6. Go through the ABCs and state at least one thing beginning with each letter that you're thankful God has given you or from which He has delivered you. (Feel free to cheat on "X" and substitute a word with "x" in it!)

Journal Entry

Please consider completing this sentence in your personal journal:

So, today I've been thinking about becoming more intentional about thanking You, Jesus, and . . .

conclusion
THE SANCTITY OF SCARS

I got to hang out with Wonder Woman last night. Well, not Wonder Woman *exactly*. Her name is Lori, not Lynda (as in Lynda Carter of *Wonder Woman* television series fame). But she's incredibly brave despite her lack of knee-high red boots and a cape. Because Lori just passed the three-month mark of being clean from methamphetamines after an eight-year addiction that culminated in her conviction for illegal drug possession and armed robbery charges.

Unlike most of the women I meet at The Next Door (a six-month residential transitional living program that provides recovery support services for women addicted to alcohol and drugs), Lori looks younger than her age (she's twenty-three). As a matter of fact, if I'd seen her strolling through the mall or giggling with her girlfriends at Starbucks, I would've assumed she was a happy-go-lucky college student. She has beautiful fair skin and big blue eyes. She was wearing a hoodie sweatshirt with a popular logo emblazoned on the front, torn jeans, and metallic nail polish. It wasn't until she pushed up her sleeves, and I noticed the long ragged scars from shooting up, that the tragic reality of her former life became apparent.

Because I've had the privilege of volunteering with several addiction-recovery programs, much of Lori's story is achingly familiar. She grew up in a very poor family in a very small town. One of her parents moonlighted as a mean-spirited bully, who smacked her around just to "knock the stupid out of her." Of course, Lori wasn't stupid at all. Despite the beatings she endured at home, she excelled in school. She made the honor role and the cheerleading squad. After making an emotional commitment to Christ at an Acquire the Fire youth event (with evangelist Ron Luce and various Christian musicians), she became an outspoken Christian leader on campus. However, when her parents divorced and she became the sole possession of her abuser, Lori's world caved in. She eventually ran away from home and moved in with her boyfriend. He introduced her to methamphetamines, which numbed the searing pain of the compound fractures in her heart. And the rest, as they say, is history. Horrible, awful, gut-wrenching history.

That is until God intervened with a few tough guys wearing flak jackets. Lori's voice brightened when she got to the part where federal agents burst into her trailer to arrest her. She looked up through her bangs and grinned. Then she said with newfound confidence, "I *know* God ordained the exact timing of my drug bust, because I'd planned to commit suicide that afternoon. If those cops hadn't come when they did, I wouldn't be sitting here today." Before I left, we talked about the Bible study we'll be doing every Wednesday night for the next three months until she has to report to prison to serve what will likely be a reduced sentence of about eighteen months. When we hugged good-bye, she whispered she wanted to be a Bible teacher too when she gets out. I told her I hoped she will be. Lori's recovery will be a day-by-day, uphill journey, but I can totally picture her a few years from now standing in front of a room filled with wide-eyed young girls hanging on her every word. What an amazing story she'll have to tell.

The older I get, the more convinced I am that admittedly flawed sinners are the most credible witnesses of Jesus, because people with scars can't fake moral perfection. It's glaringly apparent we can't save ourselves. Wounded Christian warriors with scabby knees, bruised hearts, and even track-marked arms, who sometimes stumble yet always grab onto the arm of His Spirit in order to stand up again and again, exemplify the redemptive power of divine grace. We prove how miraculous and restorative the love of God really is.

Please don't listen to the enemy when he tries to convince you it's time to wave a white flag. To cry uncle. To stop believing and talking about how good God is simply because you've made some bad mistakes. Stand back up and keep walking in faith.

It's okay if you're a little wobbly.

NOTES

Chapter 1: Ewe Scared?

1. D. A. Carson, *How Long, O Lord?* (Grand Rapids: Baker Academic, 2006), 97.

2. Dr. Daniel Doriani, "Life and Teachings of Jesus" (class lecture and syllabus notes, Covenant Theological Seminary, St. Louis, MO, January–April 2006).

Chapter 2: The Very Real Problem with Pantyhose

1. Henri Nouwen, *The Wounded Healer* (New York: Doubleday, 1979), 41.

2. Spiros Zodhiates, ed., *Hebrew-Greek Key Word Study Bible, NIV Edition* (Chattanooga, TN: AMG, 1996), 2122.

3. William Hendricksen, *New Testament Commentary: Exposition of the Gospel According to Matthew* (Grand Rapids: Baker, 1973), 516.

Chapter 3: Take a Load Off

1. Edward T. Welch, *Addictions: A Banquet in the Grave* (Phillipsburg, NJ: P&R, 2001), xvi.

Chapter 4: No Fangs Allowed

1. Francis A. Schaeffer, *The God Who Is There* (1968; repr., Downers Grove, IL: InterVarsity, 1998), 54.

Chapter 5: Cat Appreciation Day

1. Frederick Buechner, *Listening to Your Life* (New York: HarperCollins, 1992), 2.

Chapter 6: Johnny Come Lately

1. Thomas Merton, quoted by James Finley, *Merton's Palace of Nowhere* (Notre Dame, IN: Ave Maria Press, 1978), 71.

2. James Montgomery Boice, *The Parables of Jesus* (Chicago: Moody, 1983), 63.

Chapter 7: Getting Our Squeeze On

1. Philip Yancey, *What's So Amazing About Grace?* (Grand Rapids: Zondervan, 1997), 52.

2. Kenneth Bailey, *Jesus Through Middle Eastern Eyes* (Downers Grove, IL: InterVarsity, 2008), 173.

Chapter 8: The Bride Who Tripped Down the Aisle

1. Anita Renfroe, *If You Can't Lose It, Decorate It* (Colorado Springs: NavPress, 2007), 142.

2. Spiros Zodhiates, ed., *Hebrew–Greek Key Word Study Bible, NIV Edition* (Chattanooga, TN: AMG, 1996), 2049.

3. William Hendricksen, *New Testament Commentary: John* (Grand Rapids: Baker Academic, 1953), 500.

4. Spiros Zodhiates, *Hebrew–Greek Key Word Study Bible*, 2122.

5. William Hendricksen, *New Testament Commentary: John*, 500.

Chapter 9: Who's Got Your Back?

1. Donald Miller, *Blue Like Jazz* (Nashville: Thomas Nelson, 2003), 173.

2. John F. O'Grady, *Jesus, Lord and Christ* (New York: Paulist, 1973), 81.

3. *Webster's Encyclopedic Unabridged Dictionary of the English Language* (San Diego: Thunder Bay, 2001), s.v. "eschatology."

4. Lesslie Newbigin, *The Gospel in a Pluralistic Society* (Grand Rapids: Eerdmans, 1989), 222.

5. Henri J. M. Nouwen, *The Wounded Healer* (Doubleday: New York, NY, 1979), 66.

Chapter 10: Busyness Isn't a Spiritual Gift

1. Richard Foster, *Prayer, Finding the Heart's True Home* (HarperSanFrancisco, 1992), 1.

2. Wilfred A. Peterson, quoted in Tim Hansel, *When I Relax I Feel Guilty* (Elgin, IL: David C. Cook, 1979).

Chapter 11: Empathizing with Enemies

1. Brennan Manning, *Abba's Child* (Colorado Springs: NavPress, 1994), 69.

2. Anne Lamott, *Bird by Bird* (New York: Random House, 1995), 22.

Chapter 12: Liar, Liar! Pants on Fire!

1. Gerald May, *Addiction and Grace* (San Francisco: Harper and Row, 1988), 168.

2. Timothy Keller, *The Prodigal God: Recovering the Heart of the Christian Faith* (New York: Penguin, 2008), 10.

3. Ibid.

Chapter 13: Putting Down the Pen

1. G. K. Chesterton, *Orthodoxy* (John Lane Company, 1908; repr., San Francisco: Ignatius, 1995), 66.

2. Craig Blomberg, *Interpreting the Parables* (Downers Grove, IL: InterVarsity, 1990), 326–27.

3. Alan D. Wright, *Lover of My Soul* (Sisters, OR: Multnomah, 1998), 83.

Chapter 14: Carrying Home a Giant

1. Anne Lamott, *Plan B: Further Thoughts on Faith* (New York: Riverhead, 2005), 54–55.

2. C. S. Lewis, *Mere Christianity* (New York: HarperCollins, 1952), 60.

3. Sarah Young, *Jesus Calling* (Nashville: Thomas Nelson, 2004), 17.

Chapter 15: The Galvanizing Effect of Gratitude

1. Dr. Dan Allender and Dr. Tremper Longman, *Bold Love* (Colorado Springs: NavPress, 1992), 43.

2. "I Will Say," Lou Fellingham, Nathan Fellingham and busbee. Copyright © 2005 Thankyou Music & The Livingstone Collective /Adm. by worshiptogether.com Songs

excl. UK & Europe, adm. by Kingswaysongs, a division of David C Cook, tym@kingsway.co.uk. Used by permission.

3. Philip Yancey, *Where Is God When It Hurts?* (Grand Rapids: Zondervan, 1998), 23.

4. Ben Witherington III, *The Gospel of Mark: A Socio-Rhetorical Commentary* (Grand Rapids: Eerdmans, 2001), 102–3. See also Leviticus 13:45.

5. Ken Gire, *Moments with the Savior: A Devotional Life of Christ* (Grand Rapids: Zondervan, 1998), 110–11.

6. Yancey, *Where Is God When It Hurts?*, 25–26.